"Hearing God's call and choosing a life of service to the church is one of the most important, and most difficult, decisions that a person can make. The authors of *Catholics on Call: Discerning a Life of Service in the Church* offer valuable insights into religious life and vocational discernment. This book is a wonderful resource for anyone who is in the process of vocational discernment. It is equally valuable for those who know someone who is considering an ecclesial ministry. A must read."

—Rev. Martin O. Moran, III
Executive Director
The Catholic Campus Ministry Association

"Some advice for all who minister to young adults: read *Catholics on Call* with chapters by outstanding, pastorally sensitive authors (Donald Senior, Robert Schreiter, Robert Morneau, Thomas Rausch, Sheila McLaughlin, Charlene Diorka, Stephen Bevans, and Robin Ryan) who present helpful theological perspectives and practical suggestions for young adults discerning their vocation; give copies of the book to young people (it is written with them in mind) who may be interested in church ministry; form a group to discuss the book; and send some young adults to the informative and inspirational 'Catholics on Call' summer conferences run by the Catholic Theological Union in Chicago."

—James J. Bacik
Campus Minister and Adjunct Professor
University of Toledo

Catholics on Call

*Discerning a Life of Service
in the Church*

Edited by Robin Ryan, CP

LITURGICAL PRESS
Collegeville, Minnesota

www.litpress.org

	3	4	5	6	7	8

Library of Congress Cataloging-in-Publication Data

Catholics on call : discerning a life of service in the church / edited by Robin Ryan.
    p.   cm.
    Includes bibliographical references.
    ISBN 978-0-8146-3270-3 — ISBN 978-0-8146-3923-8 (e-book)
    1. Vocation, Ecclesiastical—Congresses. 2. Vocation (in religious orders, congregations, etc.)—Congresses. 3. Catholic Church—United States—Clergy—Appointment, call, and election—Congresses. I. Ryan, Robin, 1955–

BX2380.C42 2010
262'.142—dc22   2009051162

Contents

Acknowledgments

The authors of this book wish to express their gratitude to the Lilly Endowment Inc., whose generosity made the Catholics on Call program possible and whose encouragement was essential to the writing of this volume.

We are also grateful to Birgit Oberhofer, associate director of Catholics on Call, and Elizabeth Weigel, Joseph Cardinal Bernardin scholar and Catholics on Call intern, for their generosity in reviewing these chapters and offering their insights from a young adult perspective.

Robin Ryan, CP

Introduction
A New Generation of Leaders

They arrive on planes, trains, and buses from around the country. The T-shirts they wear indicate their affiliations and commitments: campus ministry associations, Bread for the World, diocesan young adult groups, international volunteer programs, Taizé prayer and eucharistic adoration groups. They are young adults discerning a life of service in the church who are gathering for an experience of reflection on their vocational journey. Some of them are at an advanced stage of discernment, having confided in a spiritual director for some time and explored a variety of options related to lay ecclesial ministry, religious life, or priesthood. Others are just beginning. They have a vague sense that God is calling them to something special, but they are uncertain about what path they should take and how to go about making the best choices for their lives. All of them—to a person—express their gratitude for the opportunity to come together with like-minded peers who are asking similar questions about their lives and are considering a call to serve the people of God. They report that they often feel alone and isolated among their friends and sometimes even among family members, who question their desire to explore an ecclesial vocation. Meeting others who have felt a similar tug from God

1

is reassuring and illuminating as they listen to their stories and learn from one another's experience.

This book emerges from the experience of young adult conferences conducted by Catholics on Call, the national vocation discovery program at Catholic Theological Union funded by the Lilly Endowment Inc. In its first four years of offering summer conferences 245 young adults have participated in programs that bring together men and women, ages eighteen to thirty, who are exploring a life of service in the church as a vowed religious, lay ecclesial minister, or priest. At these conferences young adults listen to and dialogue about presentations on call, prayer, discernment, and the various avenues of service in the church. They also visit and converse with distinguished pastoral ministers who share the stories of their own vocational discernment and the paths that led them to their ministries. These young adult discerners are accompanied by mentors who listen to their questions and dreams and facilitate discussion. All of this takes place in the context of prayer as participants share in the Eucharist, the Liturgy of the Hours, and a variety of other prayer experiences drawn from the church's rich spiritual tradition.

Young Adults and the Church

The Practice of Faith

The women and men who come to Catholics on Call are keenly aware that the relationship between the institutional church and contemporary young adults is a tenuous one. They often hear older Catholics express their concerns about the faith development and religious practice of young adults. In a 2003 poll of U.S. Catholics, more than half of those surveyed said that a lack of participation by young adults is a serious problem for the church. They listed this concern as one of the three most serious problems faced by the U.S. Catholic Church, along with the clergy sexual abuse scandal and the decline in vocations to religious life and the priesthood.[1] Catholics on Call participants realize that most of their peers do not celebrate the Eucharist on a regular basis, even though they readily identify themselves as Catholics. Their young adult friends tend not to view infrequent participation in the sacraments as a problem. Raised in a culture of choice, young adults are at home selecting elements within Catholic tradition and practice that they wish to comprise their own Catholic identity. Most of them readily espouse belief in a personal God, the incarnation, resurrection, and divinity of Jesus, the real presence of Christ in the Eucharist, and devotion to Mary. They also rate the call to reach out to the poor as among the most important Catholic teachings. At the same time, they tend to judge church teachings about frequenting the sacraments, sexual and reproductive morality, the role of women in the church, and marriage requirements as of much less significance for their Catholic identity.

Knowledge of the Tradition

Young adults associated with Catholics on Call want to know more about what it means to be Catholic. Like many young adult Catholics, they say that the formation in the faith that they received was inadequate. They claim that it was long on process and short on content, leaving them with little grasp of the tradition. In a recent study, Dean Hoge and Marti Jewell stated as one of their key findings, "Whether self-identified as traditional or liberal, young adults want to know more about their faith."[2] Catholics on Call participants remind presenters and mentors that we must not assume that teachings and practices that older Catholics have internalized are known to younger Catholics. What many older Catholics learned about their tradition "by osmosis" is not as familiar to Catholics in their twenties and thirties.

A Different Generation

The leaders of Catholics on Call have learned from young adults that they sometimes feel frustrated at the failure of middle-aged and older Catholics to understand their concerns and aspirations regarding faith and life with God. They are disillusioned by the ideological battles that have been waged by Catholics in the years since the Second Vatican Council. Classifying young adult Catholics as "liberal," "conservative," "pre–Vatican II," or "post–Vatican II" can be misleading because it projects onto young adults labels that are more descriptive of an older generation. Writing for and about the younger generation of Catholics, Tim Muldoon argues that young adults have little foundation on which to build their understanding of controversies that are at the forefront of debate among Catholics. Muldoon observes about young adults, "They have become disillusioned by the fact that so much energy is spent trying to vilify the perceived enemy, rather than building a community founded in love seeking justice."[3] Muldoon's conclusions are consonant with our experience in the Catholics on Call program. For example, some young adults who are strongly committed to the church's social justice mission are also attracted to traditional practices like eucharistic adoration and the rosary. They do not view such practices of prayer as devotional "throwbacks" but as a discovery of dimensions of the Catholic tradition that they find compelling. Many of the labels and categories employed by post–Vatican II Catholics do not align with the perspectives of Catholics in their twenties and thirties.

Interest in Church Vocations

Are contemporary young adults really interested in the prospect of undertaking lives of service in the church as religious, priests, or lay ecclesial ministers? Some observers think not; they adopt a basically negative view about these possibilities. Focusing specifically on the call to religious life, Jesuit anthropologist Richard Malloy argues that there is a radical difference—a "disconnect"—between the culture in which U.S. young adults are immersed and the values enshrined in consecrated life. He thinks that the influence of the U.S. culture on young adults makes a vocation based on the vows of poverty, chastity, and obedience seem very foreign to them.[4]

But others who are familiar with the spirituality of young adult Catholics offer a more positive view concerning the possibilities of young adults responding to a call to an ecclesial vocation. In a 2008 survey of newer members of religious communities that was conducted by the Center for Applied Research in the Apostolate, researchers concluded that "there are still significant numbers of men and women who are responding to a call to religious life and are hopeful about its future."[5] And in their 2007 survey of young adult Catholics involved in campus ministry or diocesan programs, Dean Hoge and Marti Jewell discovered a notable degree of openness to a life of service in the church.[6] One-third of the college students and nearly half of the diocesan sample said that they had seriously considered lay ecclesial ministry as a future vocation. More than 80 percent of these young adults felt that lay ministry is a call from God. Approximately half of the men in the survey reported that they had seriously considered becoming a priest at one time in their lives. While the level of current interest was more difficult to assess, Hoge and Jewell estimated that 18 percent of the men involved in campus ministry activities and 10 percent of the men engaged in diocesan programs were still interested in a vocation to ministerial priesthood. Approximately one-third of those surveyed said that they had seriously considered becoming a religious sister or brother. About 70 percent of the men and one-third of the women stated that they had been encouraged by someone to consider ministry as a priest, brother, or sister. While these findings do not augur an immediate end to what many call the "vocation crisis" in the church, they do indicate that there are young adult Catholics who are willing to consider a call to an ecclesial vocation. This study also demonstrated that the more involved young adults are in the life of their parish, diocese, or campus ministry the more likely they will be to consider such a call. The authors of the study emphasized the need for pastoral ministers to redouble their efforts in inviting young adults to active participation in the life and ministries of the church.

These findings resonate with the experience of those who have spent time with young adults in the Catholics on Call program.

There are a significant number of Catholics in their twenties and thirties who manifest a genuine interest in a life of service to the church as religious, priests, and lay ecclesial ministers. These are intelligent, thoughtful, and generous men and women, many of whom have already offered a great deal of time and energy in volunteer service through the church and other organizations, serving the most vulnerable people in our world. These young adults want to meet older Catholics who will listen to their aspirations and dreams and take them seriously. They need and appreciate assistance with their personal discernment in an environment that is free of the pressure to move in any particular direction. They are in search of experienced mentors who will accompany them and offer their wisdom for the journey. As suggested above, they also yearn to come to a deeper understanding of the Catholic tradition in its many dimensions, including its rich store of spiritual practices. And they want to hear words of invitation and encouragement assuring them that they can indeed become the next generation of leaders in the church.

About This Book

This book is directed to young adult Catholics and to pastoral ministers who work with them in the discernment of vocation. Born from the Catholics on Call experience, it seeks to introduce men and women who are considering a life of service in the church to the dynamics of vocational discernment and the different paths of life and ministry within the church. It also explains important dimensions of the Catholic tradition that are relevant to responding to God's call, such as the understanding of the nature and mission of the church. The book can be used in a variety of ways among distinct audiences. It can serve as a source of personal reading for a young adult who wants to find out more about a church vocation. It could be used as a resource for a retreat for young adults or a lecture series in a campus ministry program. A book club in a parish or campus ministry setting may find the reflections by these theologians to be a fruitful source of dialogue. Campus ministers, vocation directors, and young adult ministers will find the book to be a stimulus for dialogue about their work with young adults in vocational discernment.

We have already seen that young adults want reliable mentors who can serve as experienced guides along the journey of faith and vocation. The authors of this book have been chosen not only because of their extensive knowledge of theology and spirituality but also because they are wise mentors willing to share their own experience with a younger generation.

Donald Senior, a Passionist biblical scholar and the president of Catholic Theological Union, helps readers become immersed in the meaning and dynamics of vocation as disclosed in the Scriptures. His intriguing survey of biblical vocation stories makes it clear that God calls ordinary people to extraordinary service and that most of these people have to struggle with doubts and hesitations in responding to the call.

Robert Schreiter, a Precious Blood Missionary and expert on issues of faith and culture, reflects on the challenges of following Jesus in the context of the cultural milieu of North America. Acknowledging that "choice" is a cherished value in our individualistic culture, Schreiter underlines the need for young people to find trustworthy sources of guidance as they sort out the dizzying array of possibilities that are available to them.

In addressing the topic of prayer, I emphasize that vocational discernment requires a commitment to make our lives an ongoing conversation with God. Those who are considering a vocation to religious life, priesthood, or lay ecclesial ministry need to develop a vital friendship with Christ—a relationship made possible by the presence and action of grace in their lives.

Bishop Robert Morneau, a well-known author and spiritual guide, introduces readers to the skills of discernment. The principles of discernment that he explains can serve as reliable guideposts for those seeking to hear and respond to God's voice.

Thomas Rausch, a Jesuit systematic theologian and experienced college professor, presents a contemporary understanding of the nature and mission of the church that is rooted in the earliest traditions of Christianity. This ecclesiology, based on the notion of communion, envisions the church as a global community of memory in which every Christian is called to a shared life in Christ with God and with others.

Sheila McLaughlin, director of the Cardinal Bernardin Center at Catholic Theological Union and a national leader in lay ministry, charts the development of lay ecclesial ministry in the church since Vatican II. She draws our attention to the importance of the 2005 statement by the U.S. bishops, Coworkers in the Vineyard of the Lord, and she explains the many ways in which laypeople serve as professional ministers within the church.

Charlene Diorka, a Sister of Saint Joseph and associate director of the National Religious Vocation Conference, offers a lucid and compelling description of the vocation to vowed religious life. Noting that religious life is a life of service, she shows how the traditional vows of poverty, chastity, and obedience lead to a countercultural way of living that frees one to be of service to God's people.

Stephen Bevans, a Divine Word Missionary priest and theologian, presents an understanding of priesthood as "a ministry for ministry." He describes the ministry of the priest as one of calling God's people to their full potential as members of the Body of Christ.

A Communion of Vocations

The calls to religious life, priesthood, and lay ecclesial ministry that are described in this book are grounded in a more fundamental vocation—the call to holiness. In its Dogmatic Constitution on the Church (*Lumen Gentium*), the Second Vatican Council taught that all the baptized are called to holiness and that this call is foundational for all other vocations within the church. The council said, "It is therefore quite clear that all Christians in any state or walk of life are called to the fullness of Christian life and to the perfection of love, and by this holiness a more human manner of life is fostered also in earthly society" (LG 40).[7] Donald Senior and Stephen Bevans each highlight this fundamental vocation of the baptized as a call that unites and binds us together as followers of Jesus, prior to any differentiation into distinct ways of life and ministry within the church. Vatican II teaches us that "all the faithful are invited and obliged to holiness and the perfection of their own state of life" (LG 42). In the Bible, the call to holiness is really about *belonging*. The people of Israel are called a holy people because they belong to the all-holy God; they are God's "special possession" (see Exod 19:3-8; NAB). In the New Testament the members of the first Christian communities were called "saints" ("holy ones") not because they were necessarily morally superior to other people but because in Christ and through baptism they belonged to God (see 1 Pet 2:9-10). Because we have died and risen with Christ in baptism, all Christians are called to remember *who* they are and *whose* they are. We are summoned to affirm the dignity that we have been given as sons and daughters of God and to live in a way that demonstrates that we belong to God. This way of holiness always entails a life of service to others in the name of Christ—ministry that takes many different forms according to one's particular vocation and context.

Thus, there is a communion of vocations within the church. Thomas Rausch describes the church as a global community, a communion of churches. This understanding of what it means to be church is one that is centered on relationship—relationship with God and others. Life as a follower of Jesus entails an ever-deepening communion with the triune God and with all those who comprise the Body of Christ in the world. Every Christian is invited to envision his or her chosen way of life as a response to God's call, and all believers are summoned to participate actively in the church's mission of proclaiming the reign of God. Whether single, married, ordained, or in religious life—and whatever occupation a person undertakes—the life and work of every Christian are meant to contribute to making the church a more radiant sign of salvation in Christ.

This same reality of communion applies to vocations that are specifically designated as "ecclesial"—religious life, priesthood, lay ecclesial ministry. Each of these distinct forms of committed service in the church witnesses to the presence of Christ and helps the church to fulfill its mission in the world. Vocations to dedicated service in the church should not be understood as a zero-sum game—as if, for example, the growth in the numbers of lay ecclesial ministers is "subtracting" from vocations to religious life and priesthood. On the contrary, these are distinct but complementary ways of serving the people of God and building up the Body of Christ. There is an urgent need for closer collaboration between religious, priests, and lay ministers in their service to God's people. Young adults who are considering these ways of life and service should envision them within the framework of a communion of vocations in the church.

The Challenges of Discernment

Two distinguished sociologists of religion have recently published important studies of the religious interests and commitments of young adults.[8] In *After the Baby Boomers*, Robert Wuthnow of Princeton University analyzes the religious beliefs and practices of contemporary young adults across faith traditions, comparing them with those of the same age cohort of the 1970s. He points out that the trend toward marrying and having children later in life has led to an extended period of single life and vocational exploration. Young adults in their twenties and thirties are exploring a multitude of options, and sometimes they feel lost as they do so. In *Souls in Transition*, Christian Smith, a researcher at the University of Notre Dame, draws similar conclusions from his study of the religious and spiritual lives of eighteen- to twenty-three-year-olds. Smith points out that "the transition from the teenage years to fully achieved adulthood has stretched out into an extended stage that is often amorphous, unstructured, and convoluted, lasting upward of 12 or more years." While these years are marked by "a lot of fun and growth" they are also characterized by "a great deal of transience, confusion, anxiety, self-obsession, melodrama, conflict, stress, disappointment, and sometimes emotional damage and bodily harm."⁹ Wuthnow voices his concern that few institutional supports exist in our society to assist men and women in this age group in making important life decisions. He says, "We cannot hope to be a strong society if we invest resources in young people until they are eighteen or twenty and then turn them out to find their way entirely on their own."¹⁰

We believe that what Wuthnow and Smith say about the overall young adult population in the United States is applicable to the situation of Catholics in their twenties and thirties. Young adult Catholics, particularly those who are considering an ecclesial vocation, need the church's ongoing support in their vocational exploration. They deserve to have experienced mentors accompany them as they attempt to discern and respond to God's call in their lives. It is the hope of each of the authors of this book that what is presented here will inform, guide, and inspire the many gifted and committed young adults who wish to give their lives in service to the church. We hope that readers of this book will find support and encouragement as they listen for God's voice and seek to respond to God's call.

1

Donald Senior, CP

Answering the Call:
Biblical Perspectives

Since the time of Jesus and his first disciples, Christians have used the metaphor of "call" or "vocation" to describe the search for God's will in their lives. What will I do with my life? Where and how will I find a life of meaning and purpose?

For people of faith, the answer to that question ultimately involves confidence that God has given each of us unique gifts and wants us to flourish in our lives. Searching the Scriptures does not give us magical answers or quick solutions but can provide us—as it has generations before us—with the courage and wisdom to seek our call in life and to respond generously.

It has always intrigued me that in biblical Hebrew the way of referring to past and future has the opposite orientation than it does in English. While we say "the past is behind me" and "the future is in front of me," the biblical idiom is the opposite: that is, "the past is in front of me" (literally, "before my face") and "the future is behind me" ("at my back"). The image is visual, something like rowing a boat across the lake. The receding shoreline is "in front of you"; where you are headed is at your back, behind you. You view the "past"—the receding shore—in order to fix your course for where you are going.

This is how the Scriptures function for us, it strikes me. We view our sacred past not out of nostalgia but to find there the footprints of God, the traces of our religious roots in order to give us direction for the future that we cannot see but that we know God holds out for us. Our Scriptures give us the images and metaphors and collective wisdom that help us find our vocation in life.

The Call Stories

Stories about those who were "called" to follow Jesus abound in the New Testament, particularly in the gospels. In the opening chapters of the gospels of Mark and Matthew, Simon and Andrew are found casting their nets in the sea along with James, son of Zebedee and John his brother, sitting in their boat mending their nets. None of them has an inkling of what is about to happen to them, something that will change their lives forever. Jesus, walking by the sea, calls to them: "Follow me and I will make you fish for people" (Mark 1:16-20). They drop their nets and leave their father and his workers behind in the boat where they had been sitting and follow Jesus.

In Capernaum, the border town on the frontier between the realms of Herod Antipas and Herod Philip, Jesus meets Levi son of Alphaeus sitting at his tollbooth and once again "Follow me" is the unadorned command. Without hesitation Levi gets up, leaves his counter, and follows Jesus. That night Jesus dines in celebration with Levi's tax collector friends and other unsavory characters, earning a sharp rebuke from the religious leaders. But Jesus does not hesitate: "Those who are well have no need of a physician, but those who are sick; I have come to call not the righteous but sinners." (Mark 2:17).

Luke's gospel has a variant on these inaugural call stories in his enticing account of the call of Peter. Jesus' magnetic power draws large crowds to the shore of the sea, thirsting to hear his words. Their eagerness presses Jesus to the water's edge where some fishermen are washing their nets, their boats now empty after a nighttime of futile fishing. Jesus steps into Simon's boat and asks him to push off a bit from the shore, and in such a glorious pulpit Jesus of Nazareth preaches to the crowds fanned out on the shoreline of the cove in front of him. His sermon finished, he asks Simon to cast out into the deep and to let down the nets for a catch. "Master," Simon replies, "we have worked all night long but have caught nothing. Yet if you say so, I will let down the nets." When the nets are full to the breaking point with fish, Simon Peter, overwhelmed, falls down at Jesus' knees and exclaims, "Go away from me, Lord, for I am a sinful man." Jesus responds, "Do not be afraid; from now on you will be catching people." When the boat comes to shore, Simon and his partners James and John leave everything and follow Jesus (Luke 5:1-11).

John's gospel presents the inaugural calls differently, as is often the case with the Fourth Gospel. The call of Jesus comes not as a command by the shore of the sea or at a tollbooth in Galilee, but in the Judean desert in the southern part of Israel. While John the Baptist is preaching to his disciples, Jesus passes by like some haunting specter. "Here is the Lamb of God who takes away the sin of the world," acclaims the Baptist. As if caught in the beauty of his net, two of John's disciples begin to follow after Jesus. Jesus turns and says to them, "What are you looking for?"—a question that echoes down the centuries like a distant clap of thunder. "Rabbi, where are you staying?" "Come and see." And so begins a chain of allurement as Andrew returns to draw Simon Peter his brother to come and see what he has seen. And then Philip and then Nathaniel—all enthralled by the mysterious power of Jesus (see John 1:35-51).

There are many other stories, some with poignant variations. In the Acts of the Apostles, Paul, so sure of his own convictions and determined to destroy the early followers of Jesus, is knocked to the ground on the way to Damascus, blinded by the brilliance of the risen Christ and called to be Christ's chosen vessel even as he kicks against the goad (Acts 9:1-9). With the help of Ananias and the other Christians in Damascus, Paul will now begin to proclaim the Gospel to the world (Acts 9:10-22).

Peter's call is renewed at the end of John's gospel, in perhaps the most exquisite story of all the New Testament. Deflated disciples fish listlessly on the Sea of Galilee, when a figure appears on the shore with a charcoal fire—someone unknown but hauntingly familiar. The mysterious figure gives directions again for where to fish and once more, as in Luke's account, there is an abundant catch. Then comes the heart-pounding recognition that it is the risen Christ who stands on the shore. Peter plunges into the sea and swims ashore to find a breakfast of bread and fish prepared. And then the moment of reconciliation: "Simon son of John, do you love me?" The threefold question heals the breach of a threefold betrayal. "Feed my lambs. . . . Tend my sheep." Here discipleship is restored and the call renewed (John 21:1-19).

Luke's account of the annunciation to Mary also serves as a type of "call" story. A voice from God on the lips of an angel calls her to a new and startling life, a life of unexpected abundance and wrenching suffering, a call to bring God's own life into the world in a manner of unimaginable beauty and daring. To this call, she says, "Here am I, the servant of the Lord; let it be with me according to your word" (Luke 1:26-38).

Not all the calls were heeded. A rich young man whom Jesus loves turns away because the cost is too high (Matt 19:16-22). For a scribe seeking the truth about the commands of the law, the call is still a distance away—"You are not far from the king-dom of God"—Jesus says to him (Mark 12:34). For Nicodemus, who dares to come to Jesus only by night, the shattering loss of Jesus' death finally moves him to overcome his fears and claim the body of the crucified Christ (John 19:39).

Qualities of the Gospel Call Stories

We might note at the outset some of the fundamental qualities of these gospel call stories. First of all, the stories make abun-dantly clear that the life of discipleship begins not with a choice but with a call. It is Jesus who either by majestic command or compelling allure initiates the life of discipleship.

Second, most of the stories also make clear that the call is first and foremost a call to follow after Jesus. The focal point is the person of Christ—that remains the heart and soul of all Christian experience.

Third, the disciples who are called to follow Jesus also will share in his mission of redemption: "I will make you fish for people." They will be plunged into the work of establishing the reign of God, of healing and exorcism and teaching just as Jesus did. And their destiny will be to encounter the withering power of alienation and death in Jerusalem just as he did, but, ultimately, to share also in the joy of his resurrection.

Finally, these stories make clear that the lives of those called will be transformed. They leave their boats and their families and their tollbooth. Once the call is heard, their lives fundamentally change and new allegiances are required.

The Old Testament and God's Call

Compelling stories about God's call that gives direction to people's lives are also found in the Old Testament. This is particularly true of the stories from the prophetic and historical literature of Israel's scriptures, where God calls human beings to follow the divine path and to participate in the drama of human redemption.

When, for example, in his letter to the Galatians (1:15), Paul the Apostle reflects on his first encounter with the risen Christ, he does not use the dramatic language of sudden conversion found in the story of the road to Damascus in the Acts of the Apostles, but the language of "call," or vocation, echoing words found in the prophet Isaiah: "The LORD called me before I was born, while I was in my mother's womb he named me. . . . I will give you as a light to the nations, that my salvation may reach to the end of the earth" (Isa 49:1-6). A similar text is found in the opening words of Jeremiah: "Before I formed you in the womb I knew you, and before you were born I consecrated you; I appointed you a prophet to the nations" (Jer 1:5).

Virtually all of the great characters who would shape the destiny of Israel receive such divine calls. God asks Abraham and Sarah who are viewed as the parents of Israel's history to set out on a journey of faith, leaving their homestead behind and, as the letter to the Hebrews would say, setting out on a journey whose destiny they did not yet know (Heb 11:8). And with exquisite beauty and even great humor the Bible makes clear that this journey of faith was not the initiative of Abraham but was a call from God. In Genesis 17 God appears to Abraham and promises the patriarch that he will be the ancestor of a multitude of nations. Abraham, dismayed at this impossible prospect, hides his face in the crook of his elbow and laughs—"Can a child be born to a man who is a hundred years old? Can Sarah, who is ninety years old, bear a child?" (Gen 17:17).

The saga is repeated in the next chapter of Genesis when three mysterious visitors appear at the tent of Abraham and Sarah at Mamre near Hebron. Abraham recognizes that these visitors are the divine presence and so he prepares a feast for them. When they are about to leave, they repeat the preposterous promises: Sarah will bear a child and the offspring of Abraham and Sarah will be as numerous as the stars. Standing behind the tent flap, Sarah laughs at the prospect! And the Lord through the visitors challenges her: "Why did Sarah laugh? . . . Is anything too wonderful for the LORD?" (Gen 18:13-14).

There is this note of the preposterous in virtually all of the biblical call stories in both the Old and New Testaments. Moses encountering God in the burning bush at Horeb the mountain of God, hesitant and fearful as God anoints him to lead the people out of slavery: "O my Lord, I have never been eloquent, neither in the past nor even now that you have spoken to your servant; but I am slow of speech and slow of tongue." Then the Lord said to him, "Who gives speech to mortals? Who makes them mute or deaf, seeing or blind? Is it not I, the LORD? Now go, and I will be with your mouth and teach you what you are to speak" (Exod 4:10-12).

Or the call of the prophets: Amos of Tekoa, dragooned by God into a powerful mission of justice. "I am no prophet," he says, "nor a prophet's son; but I am a herdsman and a dresser of sycamore trees, and the LORD took me from following the flock, and the LORD said to me, 'Go, prophesy to my people Israel'" (Amos 7:14-15). Or Jeremiah, tongue-tied, hesitant—"I am only a boy," he tells God. "Do not say, 'I am only a boy,'" God thunders, "for you shall go to all to whom I send you, and you shall speak whatever I command you. Do not be afraid of them, for I am with you to deliver you, says the LORD" (Jer 1:6-8). Or Isaiah himself, standing in the portals of the temple overwhelmed by a sense of God's presence and his own unworthiness, crying out, "I am lost, for I am a man of unclean lips, and I live among a people of unclean lips." A seraph purifies his troubled heart with a burning coal from the temple brazier and then the voice of God penetrates the prophet's dread: "Whom shall I send, and who will go for us?" His anguish put aside, the prophet speaks: "Here am I; send me!" (Isa 6:1-9). And so it would be with all of the great characters who form the biblical saga, men and women hesitant and awkward, yet called by God to take up their mission on behalf of the people.

The call of God is often disruptive, breaking into ordinary lives and asking ordinary people to bear a mission of human transformation and to experience profound and sometimes wrenching change in order to be faithful to that divine summons. And nowhere in the Christian Bible is this more apparent than in the gospel portrayal of the disciples of Jesus. Despite their initial response to drop everything and follow him, they prove to be awkward, slow to learn, often confused. The gospel literature does not hesitate to portray the disciples at their worst: impeding Jesus' mission, objecting to his destiny in Jerusalem, and when the terrible threat of the passion fell over Jesus' ministry, deserting him, denying him, and even betraying him. Only after the death and resurrection of Jesus are the disciples reinstated in their mission and their betrayal of Jesus reconciled.

The Biblical Call Stories and the Christian Vocation

What do these biblical call stories tell us about our own search to find what we should do with our lives in today's world?

First of all, the stories remind us that the notion of vocation in its most fundamental meaning is not defined by any specific role or function but is something far greater, with God as its author and life as its subject. Sometimes in the past people thought of a call or vocation solely as applying to a commitment to priesthood or religious life. But, as important as these ways of life are, the biblical notion of vocation or call has a much broader and deeper meaning. Vocation touches upon the very foundations of our faith. We believe that God calls all human beings into life and gives them meaning and purpose, along with the freedom to choose and to commit to the gifts that God offers. That is the foundation of all the meanings of the word "call" or "vocation" in a Christian sense. As people of faith we are called throughout our lives to seek the face of God—a call to holiness and the fullness of life itself. This is the end point of the biblical quest: to see the face of God and live. It is for this that we are called, all of us as part of the human family, and surely all of us as part of the church.

This wider sense of vocation was one of the defining moments of the Second Vatican Council as it tried to express a new consciousness of what the church is, an expression that ultimately bore fruit in the council document *Lumen Gentium*, the Dogmatic Constitution on the Church. The church, it proclaimed, is the mystery of God's loving presence in the world, calling all people to holiness and fullness of life. The first definition of the church's character is not its differentiation into specific structures and roles but its common character as the pilgrim people of God, called into being by God's love and setting out on the quest for holiness and union with God. Only as a second moment—and only in service to the church's fundamental vocation to holiness and communion—can we differentiate roles within the church. This fundamental vocation is sealed in baptism. The waters of the sacrament symbolize that heritage of abundant life given by God in Christ, and also symbolize our common life and destiny with God's people.

Second, if we accept that God through Christ is the source of every vocation—the vocation of life itself and every specific aspect of our lives, including that of priesthood and consecrated life and forms of lay church service—then we should approach this question full of hope and expectation. God is with our world and with our church. In spite of ourselves, if need be, God will call people of goodwill to carry out the divine mission in the world and people will respond.

Third, we can take heart from so many of these biblical call stories because they show us that God calls ordinary people like us—people who hesitate, who are skeptical or doubt, who feel unworthy, who are unsure of their gifts, who wonder if they are making the right choice. The list is long: Abraham and Sarah thinking they are too old and that their time had passed; Moses who stammered and wondered if he could speak in public; Jeremiah who thought he was too young for the job; Isaiah who felt he was "unclean" and not worthy of the service to which God was calling him; Amos who declared that neither he nor his family was equipped for what God was asking of him; the awkward apostle Peter asking Christ to leave him alone; Mary, a young woman unsure and fearful of what God might have in store for her; and Paul, wrongheaded and stubborn, violently persecuting the followers of the very Jesus who would call him to be the Apostle to the Gentiles. All of these great characters felt inadequate for the lives of greatness to which God was calling them, but ultimately through God's grace they found the courage to respond. The very human characters in these stories encourage us never to count ourselves out.

There is another key characteristic of vocation we can draw from our biblical heritage. A Christian vocation, whatever form it takes, is inherently missionary in character with the transformation of the world as its purpose. The fishermen on the shores of the Sea of Galilee were called to become fishers of people. Peter's reconciliation on that same shore after the passion of Jesus led to the mandate to feed Christ's lambs, feed his sheep. Through baptism all Christians are called to share in the mission of Jesus—healing and teaching and reconciling and giving life and freedom to the children of God. Every expression of Christian vocation, whether in some explicit form of church service or in the professional life of medicine or science or politics or business or the art of raising a family, has a public character and a missionary purpose. Like the very being of Jesus, vocation is a call to engender life—in one's self and in the world in which God has placed us. We are called to use our gifts and energy on behalf of others, to make our world a place of beauty and justice—as God intended it to be.

Finally, the biblical call stories remind us that responding to God's vocation requires conversion and lifelong personal transformation. One has to be attentive to God's call, ready to leave something or someone behind in order to be free to follow Jesus: damp nets, a confused father, a tax collector's booth, memories of failure, a tired body, competing obligations, the tug of family and possessions, fear of the unknown and untried. Sometimes the burden to be shed is massive. The example of Peter on the shore of the Sea of Galilee during that breakfast with the risen Christ is vivid. He had to come to grips with the fact that he had publicly denied the one he loved and the one who had given every ounce of meaning to his life. "Yes, Lord, you know that I love you." The words are full of heartbreak but they had to be said before the apostle could be reinstated. Paul too had to put behind him his cocksure understanding of God's ways, a surety that had led him to persecute the church of God. He finally had to see himself not as a super apostle but as one "untimely born" (see 1 Cor 15:8-10), a frail earthen vessel carrying God's treasure (2 Cor 4:7-12). Only then could Paul be free to bring the gospel to the world.

The Journey of Discipleship

It is not by accident that the most pervasive biblical symbol for describing the life of faith is that of the "journey." Israel's history is cast as a long and often tortuous journey of faith: from the first stirrings of Abraham's trek into the pastures of Canaan, through the exodus from Egypt and the journey to the Promised Land, and from the wrenching experience of exile to a muted and hope-filled return to the land of Judah. And so too the gospels portray the life and mission of Jesus as a long journey, beginning with his ministry in Galilee and then on to the ominous and purposeful journey to Jerusalem where he would meet his destiny in death and resurrection.

The gospels are clear that this journey of Jesus and his disciples captures the spirit of the Christian experience of faith. Luke is most explicit—the first name given to the church is the "Way" or the "Journey" (see Acts 9:2; 19:23; 22:4; 24:14, 22). Response to God's call is not an instantaneous or static reality but one that unfolds over time and one that must endure the rigors of the march to Jerusalem, a journey that often involves loss, fatigue, and failure before the discovery of abundant and joyful life.

At the same time, this is not a solitary journey. The search for God's will in our lives takes place in the context of the Christian community as a whole. We are a pilgrim people, together searching to find our answer to God's call. We need to listen to the experience and guidance of others; we need to sound out our possible life choices with people we trust—our families, our friends, our spiritual advisors. We need to fortify our search with prayer and deep reflection.

The Biblical Heritage and Vocations Today

Has there ever been a time in our collective memory when there has been more need for those willing to use their gifts to bring life to our world? In a world filled with violence and with increasing chasms of hostility between cultures and races and ideologies, is there not an urgent need to demonstrate that it is possible for diverse peoples to live together in harmony and love—that community is possible through God's grace? To witness in a public way for a whole generation that thirsts for authentic spirituality that a life of holiness and virtue is indeed possible in our time? To be willing to take up those forms of service that so often governments and private agencies are tempted to abandon: working with victims of AIDS, feeding the hungry, throwing in one's lot with the homeless and abandoned, standing with the immigrant and refugee, demonstrating for peace? In a world where so much greed and dishonesty has robbed people of their livelihoods and homes and caused so much human suffering, has there ever been more need for those who will use their talents and their gifts of honesty and integrity to build up our world, to promote justice and the common good? In a world where so many people thirst for meaning and something worthwhile to believe in, has there ever been more need for those who are willing to preach the Gospel and to bring the life of Christ to those who hunger for spiritual nourishment?

This is not an easy time for the church. Vocations to the priesthood, especially in the Western world, remain few. Many religious communities in the United States and elsewhere find themselves in a time of diminishment—consolidating and cutting back. Preparing for lay ecclesial ministry can be costly and the financial rewards cannot compare with the opportunities in business.

What do we do at a time like this? Is not this a time when we have to dig deep into our heritage and lift up again for ourselves and for the people we serve the most noble and sacred ideals of our Christian faith? We must remember with accuracy and intensity the beauty of the gospel and the highest ideals of the Christian call as priests or religious or committed laity on behalf of God's people.

From a host of recent sociological studies of young adults, we know that this new generation of Christians is no less good, no less generous, no less children of God than any previous generation before them. Only if we passionately believe in the church and its ministry, only if we believe with all our hearts that God will not abandon us and that God will call us to life, will we be able to speak without embarrassment or hesitation to young Christians and invite them to hear God's call to bring the Gospel to the world. Only when we summon up our own best ideals and deepest faith, will we be worthy of this new generation of Christians who seek a life of holiness.

For Reflection

- What do you think of when you hear the word "vocation"?
- Which biblical story of call do you most identify with?
- In what ways have you experienced God's presence and call at key moments in your journey of discipleship?

Scripture Passages

Exodus 3:1–4:17	Isaiah 6:1-8	Jeremiah 1:4-10
Luke 5:1-11	John 21:1-19	Galatians 1:11-24

Recommended Reading

Brueggemann, Walter. *The Word that Describes the World: The Bible and Discipleship*. Minneapolis: Augsburg, 2006.

O'Collins, Gerald. *Jesus: A Portrait*. Maryknoll, NY: Orbis, 2008.

Orsuto, Donna. *Holiness*. New York: Continuum, 2006.

Senior, Donald. *Jesus: A Gospel Portrait*. Rev. ed. New York: Paulist Press, 1992.

2

Robert Schreiter, CPPS

The Challenge
of Christian Discipleship
in North American Culture

Following Christ and serving the church always take place in a concrete time and place. It is one thing to be a Christian in a country where the majority profess Christian faith and an atmosphere of religious tolerance exists; it is quite another to live out one's faith as a beleaguered minority in a hostile environment. Hence it is important to look at the environment in which faith is lived out: the social, political, and economic dimensions as well as general characteristics of the age group under consideration. This chapter sets out to do that. It begins by looking at the dominant culture in the United States from a number of angles. Then it moves to some of the demographic characteristics of young adults in the United States today, with a special focus on young adult Catholics. It concludes by examining some of the challenges of a life of discipleship in the dominant culture of the United States and what that means for a church vocation today.

Facts and Features of U.S. Culture

The United States is the third-most multicultural country in the world (after Australia and Canada, which have much smaller populations). One out of every five households uses a language other than English for day-to-day communication. Among young adults, the multicultural reality is even more pronounced because of the higher birth rates among immigrant populations. Young adults have responded to this reality by exhibiting a higher tolerance of cultural and racial differences than older age groups in the population. They have grown up with this diversity and seem more at ease with it.

At the same time, there is a powerful dominant culture in the country, shaped by two hundred years of history. This culture is white, owes much to the nation's origin as a British colony, and is generally Protestant in temperament and character. It is highly individualist in outlook and considers individual choice as one of its highest values. Each person is expected to construct his or her own life, irrespective of one's family background. More will be said about this below.

For young adults, there is an additional force at work in this dominant culture. That is a youth culture that it shares in some measure with many other people of their age group around the world, especially in developed countries. This youth culture is influenced by a host of material and artistic factors. A worldwide youth culture began to develop in the 1960s when today's young adults' parents were teenagers. Such a culture has persisted, although it has continued to change as successive generations have come of age. It is marked by a common, informal mode of dress and especially by familiarity with continuing developments of technology that have changed patterns of communication and interactive association—from the advent of video games in the 1970s to Facebook, texting, and Twittering in the first decade of the twenty-first century. Perhaps the most pervasive cultural force, however, is music. Here influences from many cultures come into play.

Within these cultural flows—a historical one that grows out of traditions that mark the United States especially, and a material and artistic one that changes more rapidly—we can begin to focus on some specific features that mark U.S. society. Specifically, we will look at religion and the larger set of values that shapes the dominant culture today.

Views of Religion

When one looks at societies across the world today that have achieved significant amounts of economic well-being and a sense of general security (physical safety, long-term stability, assurance of health care, and assistance in old age), one sees that religious practice tends to decline. This phenomenon, known as "secularization," is evident especially in Western Europe, parts of North America, Australia, and New Zealand. People's daily focus is much more on the here-and-now, rather than the future. They may maintain beliefs about God and the afterlife, but they seldom find themselves engaged in prayer and worship. Religion retreats from the public square and becomes a matter of private choice. In Europe, the great cathedrals and churches remain, but more as historical and cultural monuments. Religion as such has little day-to-day impact on people's lives. Interest may increase during moments of personal crisis (such as death of a loved one), but it generally recedes once the crisis has passed. Sociologists once predicted that as societies around the world modernized and became wealthier, secularization would become more and more the social norm, and religion would be relegated to private choice and would, eventually, disappear altogether.

This pattern surely holds in many of the developed countries in the West. The big exception to this is the United States. Secularization has certainly made inroads in this country. A 2009 poll revealed that 15 percent of Americans now claim no religious faith at all—the highest number since polling of opinion began in this country. But the majority of the U.S. population maintains a higher level of religious belief and practice than in other developed Western countries, including neighboring Canada. Sociologists have puzzled about just why the United States is such an exception to the other countries most like it. Different reasons have been proposed. Some say that, because the churches in the United States receive no state support (as they do in many countries in Europe), they are more entrepreneurial and competitive. Pastors work harder to build up their congregations, as the success of "megachurches" in suburban areas seems to suggest. Others note that the United States is a nation of immigrants, and immigrants typically have a stronger sense of religious belief, especially if they have been religious minorities or have been persecuted in their home countries. Yet others suggest that U.S. culture promotes voluntary associations. Since families tend not to include extensive networks of cousins, uncles, and aunts, people find their belonging in groups they join, and churches and other religious institutions have profited from this. There is no consensus on just why this country has remained more religious, both in beliefs and in practice (somewhere between 25 and 40 percent of Americans claim they worship at least weekly, and some 70 percent say they pray or read the Bible almost every day). But the fact of such high participation has meant that religion remains a more public factor. Where the president and his family worship on Sunday is a matter of public interest—something that does not happen in other secularized societies. People feel more free to talk about their faith and religious experience here than in other such societies. Even though there is a clear separation of church and state, religion is prominent in politics. Two-thirds of Americans say that they would not vote for a presidential candidate who is an atheist.

What this means is that, even though religious leaders will decry the growing secularity of U.S. society (and it does seem to be growing), this country remains highly religious. As we shall see, this does not automatically translate into regular church attendance and ongoing commitment to a single parish or congregation. But it creates a different baseline in this country for young adults who want to deepen their religious faith and seek out a form of church ministry.

Values

Religious leaders will often speak out about a decline in values that are to be held in common. Secular societies promote more individualist approaches to values and to living and, as a result of this, shared values may seem to become obscured or even disappear. As a society becomes more economically and socially secure, a set of commonly held values necessary for mutual survival becomes less and less self-evident. If one looks to surveys on values that have been conducted over an extended period of time, such as the European Values Survey or the World Values Survey, one does indeed see a continued decline in shared value systems in secularized societies.

Again, the United States has been, up to this point, an exception. While a marked change can be seen in many Western European societies, the same has not been the case here. There were significant shifts in the 1960s, but studies suggest that the value system in the United States has been relatively stable since the early 1980s. Values around family, work, and behavior codes in society have generally been more conservative in the United States than in much of Europe, except in the area of the role of women in society, where the United States showed more egalitarian stands earlier than across the Atlantic. An increasing pluralism, however, has brought a greater sense of tolerance in its wake, providing basic economic and social security is not threatened. This tolerance is often an uncritical one of "live and let live" without much effort to evaluate the relative merit of different positions on family, sexuality, work, politics, and religion.

Perhaps the fact that the United States has remained more overtly religious than many countries in Europe accounts for less slippage in values over time. Some of the slippage experienced here today must be looked at carefully. Young adults today tend to marry and start families at a later age than in the past. As a result, they have a longer period of quest and experimentation in their twenties and into their thirties than has been the case in previous generations. This exploration can give the impression that traditional values are being set aside or even jettisoned. What is important to look at is what values are considered most important as people start families. What values do they want their children to have? Here is a better indicator of the values held in common by a society than making the period of exploration the benchmark.

While a great deal of attention has been given to shifts in values or a dissolution of any consensus about them, it pays to look at certain enduring features that are emerging from secularized societies. In a longitudinal study of values encompassing more than forty nations over a period of nearly thirty years, sociologist Ronald Inglehart has suggested that there is a pattern of values that emerges for people whom he calls "post-survival," that is, people who live in basic economic and social security. Three stand out in particular.

The first is a *quest for meaning*. When people are not preoccupied with where they will sleep tonight, where their next meal is coming from, and how they will meet the bills coming due this month, they are freed up to think about the larger questions of what it means to be a human being: just why am I here at all? Is there a larger meaning to the universe and to my own life? Why is there so much suffering in the world? What happens to me when I die? Is there a God and, if so, what difference does God make in my life? Not everyone asks these questions, nor does everyone do so all the time. But they are especially important for post-survival young adults who are trying to get their bearings and make decisions about their lives.

The second is a *distrust of institutions*. This arises out of a certain paradox. On the one hand, no institution is without its shortcomings, and rarely can these institutions meet the needs of individuals (and individualist needs) completely. Hence, they are experienced as potentially oppressive. In the United States, where some of our ancestors fled societies with especially oppressive institutions, this distrust of institutions has been passed down through the generations.

On the other hand, no society of any complexity can survive without institutions. In many of the secularized societies, the institutions that have been developed are themselves stable and create a stable and secure environment in their respective societies. They come to be taken for granted. One can "distrust" them with very little personal cost. One only has to experience a society that has no social services, where corruption is rampant and expected, or where institutions serve only the interests of a wealthy elite to the detriment of the rest of the population to realize how important good institutions are. In other words, a distrust of institutions is to some extent a luxury that wealthy societies can afford. This does not mean that one should be uncritical and accepting of how institutions in wealthy societies present themselves; critical thinking continues to be necessary, as the lessons of the 2008 financial collapse in the United States and elsewhere show. But this distrust should not be allowed to become a naïve belief that complex societies can survive without institutions.

The third is a *concern for the physical environment.* This is certainly very characteristic of the current generation of young adults, who have grown up amid the debates about climate change. There is a realization that, without the survival of the planet, there is no survival for us at all. Young adults can expect to see in their lifetimes changes that may restrict and harm life on earth. Consequently, ecological awareness is a hallmark of this generation.

Concern for the environment has another dimension as well. In a postmodern situation, where overarching ideas and stories have been treated with suspicion, concern for the earth becomes an acceptable kind of overarching story. It can provide today a common vision and common cause for a wide group of people that metaphysics and religious belief systems did in an earlier age. One may debate whether this is a good way to proceed, but it does provide a common basis in a pluralist society for common action and an ordering of shared values.

Some Characteristics of Young Adults Today

It is of course dangerous to generalize about any age group or large population. There is always a great deal of variety within any group—so much so that the differences within a group may exceed the differences between groups. Yet those who study populations have been able to offer some general characteristics of generational groups that are helpful for understanding trends within societies, as well as certain characteristics that come to the fore.

As a starting point, those who study populations say that it is important to look at what is happening in the larger world as a generation comes of age, that is, when they are in their late teens and early twenties. The experience of larger events becomes a lens through which they tend to view the world. This lens becomes a filter through which subsequent events are interpreted in the course of their lives. To be sure, such a lens may either sharpen or distort what someone sees. Generally, if people are not able to adjust their lenses over the course of a lifetime, they run the risk of becoming reactionaries—either of the Right or the Left—and will be perceived by others as "out of touch" with the meaning of a given time.

To give some examples: the generation of Americans who came of age during the Great Depression of the 1930s and World War II (parents of the so-called Baby Boomers) experienced economic scarcity and much uncertainty. In their adult years, they tended to be cautious and not willing to trust that the future would be better than the present. They placed high value on living frugally and saving for the future. Their children—born between 1946 and 1964—are generally known as the Baby Boomers, since there was a sharp increase in the number of children born during this period. They constituted the single largest age cohort or group in American history. They grew up in a time of economic abundance and optimism. As they came of age in the late 1960s, they put the whole country through a kind of adolescence with great cultural upheaval. Because their numbers are so large, their immediate concerns continue to define the social agenda even to this day.

Young adults today (roughly speaking, those born in the 1980s) have called themselves the Millennials, since they were coming of age at the turn of the third millennium. This was a time of prosperity (unlike the period of Generation X, who came of age during the recessions of the 1970s). Millennials have been described as highly altruistic, concerned about justice and service to others, and more racially and culturally tolerant than previous generations. They appear to be more reflective and concerned about the meaning of life and are willing to entertain the deeper questions that go with such a quest. They are more interested in religion and spirituality than the previous two generations.

Unlike the Boomers, who led a revolt against the established values and traditions of their parents yet internalized much of the structure that they rejected on the outside, the Millennials have lived their lives in the wake of the cultural shifts that began in the late 1960s. They are interested in lasting values, but have difficulty finding them since these values tend to be heavily obscured in American society. "Choice" is one of the highest values in the individualist culture of America. Each person is expected to construct his or her own life. That means choosing not only a life partner and an occupation but also whether to continue in the religious faith of their childhood, as well as a host of other choices. The choices made by one's parents are not indicative of what the Millennials will choose. In a culture of relative abundance, all options are to be explored.

One of the opportunities, but at the same time an obstacle, is the sheer amount of choices possible and the difficulty of seeing clearly what the consequences of the bundle of choices one makes will have on one's further life. There is precious little source of guidance in this regard. Think of the matter of choosing a college or university for middle-class high school graduates and the elaborate rituals enacted each spring as they visit school after potential school. Choosing a major once one is enrolled, and seeking a path of employment thereafter, is also more complicated for young people today than it was a generation ago. A significant number of young adults, both out of their willingness to help others but also out of an uncertainty where to go next on life's path, will devote a year or two to some social service after graduating from college. All in all, the period between finishing college and settling into marriage and family is now longer than it has been at any moment in earlier American history. This is happening not because young adults are less mature emotionally than earlier generations; it is generated in large part by the huge amount of choices that confront them and the lack of any clear guidance from the culture as to how to proceed.

In 2008, a steep economic downturn began in the United States and spread throughout the world. At this writing it is unclear how deep it will go and how long it will last. But if coming of age under these conditions mirrors similar situations from the past, the needs for survival will mute the quest for meaning as options narrow for many.

But to return to the main point: deep down, America's values do not appear to have shifted significantly over the past thirty years. Yet nearer the surface, there is a great deal of turbulence, and it is hard for those young adults in the process of shaping their mature identities to find points of orientation. From a religious point of view, mainline Protestant faith, which has been the defining cultural form of religious faith in the United States since early in the nineteenth century, has been losing its hold. Today mainline denominations (Episcopalians, Methodists, Lutherans, Presbyterians, and the like) constitute only thirteen percent of the Christian population. They have been losing members to the Evangelical churches. These more conservative brands of Christianity help provide more answers to the quests for meaning than do the mainline denominations, which often focus more on making people comfortable with living with the questions than providing answers. The Roman Catholic Church remains the largest single Christian body in the United States, with 24 percent of the population. It continues to grow slightly, but that is largely due to the arrival of Catholic immigrants, who in turn tend to have larger families (about a third of all Catholics are now of Hispanic descent). At the same time, it is important to realize that if former Catholics were to be regarded as a "denomination," they would be the second largest single Christian body in the country.

Catholics in the United States maintained loyalty to their church in numbers far beyond those in Europe through much of American history. This was because the parish was a powerful socializing factor. The decision to create an alternative school system alongside that of public schools meant that those children who attended them could be in a strongly Catholic environment from kindergarten through college. Parishes were centers for European immigrants to become Americans, yet live and marry among other Catholics. All of this helped create a rich Catholic "culture" within (and sometimes consciously against) the larger American (and predominantly Protestant) culture. Being Catholic was more than subscribing to a certain set of teachings. There were common practices and identity markers (no meat on Fridays, fasting in Lent) that helped create a powerful sense of belonging.

Starting especially in the 1960s—and at the same time as the cultural upheavals of the latter part of that decade—the boundaries of that distinctively Catholic culture began to become more porous and permeable. After the Second World War, a larger number of Catholics started attending college for the first time and began a rapid entry into the middle class. By the mid-1980s, young Catholics had the highest level of education and the highest mean incomes of any Christian group. What that meant was that being Catholic was no longer as distinctive in Protestant America as it had once been. There no longer is a Catholic "vote" that can be delivered at election time as there once was. The great advantage of this is that Catholics are not discriminated against in U.S. society as they once were. Catholics now "belong." The majority of the justices on the Supreme Court now are Catholics, where having even one Catholic on the Supreme Court would have been unimaginable a hundred years ago. But the downside is that it is harder for many people to discover and hold on to distinctive features of Catholic identity or to find a home in what was once a rich Catholic culture. That culture had many oppressive qualities to be sure, some of which need not be retrieved. But often now the richness and the coherence of Catholic faith are hard to grasp as Catholics have been assimilated into the cultural mainstream. And despite postmodern claims for the "death of the grand narrative," most people continue to search for wholeness and coherence to their lives, something that the very "Catholicity" (one of the meanings of "catholic" is "universal") of our faith holds out for us.

Many young adults are in search of that sense of a wholeness that shows the meaning and the meaningfulness of their lives. There is a sense that Catholic faith can offer such an overarching vision.

Challenges to Discipleship Today

To believe in Jesus and to take up a life of discipleship is a challenge at every time. It is always a matter, on the one hand, of finding a place to belong and call home, and a framework of belief and practices out of which to live and make sense of the world and on the other hand, of not simply being absorbed into the surrounding environment but living both critically and faithfully to what is most important. Much of the rest of the world has a love-hate relationship with the United States. On the one hand, people see this country as a place of opportunity to find a better life for themselves and their families. They are sometimes dazzled by its wealth and social power. On the other hand, they have seen the United States act so selfishly to promote its own interests at the expense of those of others that they are repelled by America's arrogance and greed. Living out a life of discipleship takes place at the crossroads of that ambivalence: of seeking a home but naming its oppressive qualities; of gaining opportunity but not at the egregious expense of others.

What are the signposts of discipleship in U.S. culture today? Let me suggest five.

Living in a Powerful Country in Uncertain Times

The events of 9/11 at the beginning of the first decade of the new millennium awoke Americans to how fragile their physical safety could be. The economic downturn at the end of that first decade did the same for their economic well-being and security. In a way, of course, Americans were simply discovering what is the daily existence of much of the rest of the world that struggles with safety and survival. These two wake-up calls, however, are an opportunity to remind ourselves of what is most central and basic to our human existence. The accumulation of goods, Jesus reminded the young man in the gospels, can be a hindrance to entering the reign of God (Matt 19:20-22). This is not because material goods are inimical to Christian existence, but they can lure us into idolatry, that is, placing our values in the wrong place. We must lay up treasures that do not rust and rot.

When uncertainty strikes the powerful, they will tend to lash out against others less powerful than themselves, or take from others so as to maintain their own advantage. A concrete case in point for the United States at this point in history is immigration. In difficult times there will be calls to halt immigration, forgetting that nearly all Americans are themselves descendants of immigrants (the exceptions are native peoples and people of African descent brought here forcibly as slaves). To their credit, according to polls taken in late 2008, Catholics overwhelmingly support the pro-immigration policies of the Catholic bishops.

Divisions in Church and Society

Highly pluralist societies are prone to all kinds of divisions. Some of these can be creative opportunities to think through new possibilities. When divisions occur in times of uncertainty, they can lead to polarizing positions that diminish everyone's sense of self and identity. The advances in communications technologies have made it possible for people to escape the rough-and-tumble world of diversity and find niches or enclaves of the like-minded. So people choose a narrower range of news media outlets and seek out like-minded people with their blogs or their social contacts.

Such hunkering down in enclaves—like a social world of gated communities—diminishes the human spirit. The 2008 national elections seemed to give some indication that people were becoming weary of constant attempts to divide people against one another and live out of narrow, single-issue identities.

What is happening in the larger society is also happening in the church. Attempts to narrow definitions of what it is to be

Catholic to a single set of issues is very "un-Catholic." Being Catholic involves embracing the whole. And to embrace the whole is to engage not in relativism but in humility—a humble awareness that we all are sinners and our grasp of our faith is always finite. We deepen that grasp not by shouting at one another but by struggling together to achieve greater faithfulness.

Many young adults are particularly weary of the endless debates of preceding generations about the meaning of the Second Vatican Council and who is truly a Vatican II Catholic. Key to overcoming divisions is how we tell our stories—the stories of who we are, the stories of what has happened. As long as we tell those stories in such a way that there are winners and losers, the faithful and the deviant, the good and the bad, we will remain in division. The story has to be retold in such a way that both parties can recognize themselves and their own struggles within the story, including our strengths and our failings. A key part of discipleship for young people today is to help older generations of Catholics overcome their bickering and find out how they are "citizens with the saints and also members of the household of God, built upon the foundation of the apostles and prophets, with Christ Jesus himself as the cornerstone" (Eph 2:19-20).

The Search for Truth

Truth is often hard to find in a pluralist society, and it is unlikely to be found when determining where the truth is means listening to who can shout the loudest. But because truth may be hard to find does not mean that we can give up the quest. To give up seeking the truth runs the risk of acquiescing to living with lies. In a noisy society with many competing voices, it is important to remember two things. First of all, to know the truth is to know more than the facts. The Truth and Reconciliation Commission that met in South Africa after the fall of apartheid has taught the world a valuable lesson. Along with objective truth, you need existential truth, that is, truth that answers the "why" questions and not just the "who" and "what" questions. You also need what they called dialogical truth, that is a truth that is capacious enough to hold the competing stories and claims—not out of a sense of relativism, but out of a sense of humility and respect for human dignity and fragility. Second, our faith teaches us that truth is a Person: "I am the way, and the truth, and the life," said Jesus (John 14:6). In the Hebrew Scriptures, the word "truth" (*'emet*) means reliability, dependability, trustworthiness. That is why God is truth. To know truth, one must be more than smart or clever. One must be attuned to the God who is the source of all truth, especially that deepest truth that holds the world together.

Individualism, Quests, Commitments

Robert Wuthnow, one of the most astute observers of American religion, once proposed that religious people today tend to be either "nesters" or "questers." Nesters seek in religion a safe haven, a home, a place to belong. They may not be as outward-looking as they need to be, but they know something about some of the deepest desires of the human heart, some that a rank individualism cannot satisfy. He suggests that the parents of the Baby Boomers were largely nesters, and that this characterized American religion in the 1950s.

Questers, on the other hand, are seekers. They are restless souls that search the terrain for sparks of the divine and glimpses of the deepest possibilities of humanity. A pluralist and individualist society, where nothing seems to be stable and durable, encourages a quester mentality and lifestyle. Wuthnow suggests that Boomers and Millennials are especially of this type.

It is important to recognize that both mentalities are part of a genuine discipleship. Especially in John's gospel, Jesus urges the disciples to come and to abide with him (John 15:4). But elsewhere, Jesus also bids the disciple to leave all things behind and come follow him into the unknown.

What both nesting and questing require is commitment. Being an individual in a pluralist society often means running away from commitment. Commitment can be made to be understood as premature foreclosing of your options. What if something or someone better comes along? What if what I have chosen doesn't work out? While these are understandable responses, by not making a commitment a person misses one of the most important things that commitment can teach us. Commitment is not just about what we choose. It is also about the experience of making a choice and sticking with it. It is often when maintaining a commitment becomes difficult that we find out the most about life and about ourselves. We come up against the finitude of all things and learn to live with it, rather than jumping to something else in the hopes of finding some illusive wholeness that probably does not exist. Having to keep a commitment even when it is difficult teaches us something about ourselves—about the ability to transcend our own limits. When we fail in commitments, we again can learn things about ourselves that our successes can never teach us. Failure can not only teach us about our own limitations but also make us more forgiving of the failures of others.

Justice, Care for Others, Compassion

Individualism, left to itself, can insulate and isolate us from the suffering and needs of others. One of the strengths many have noted in the Millennials is their heightened sense of justice and compassion. The individualism that has shaped the American Republic from its earliest years has often turned a blind eye to those who are at the bottom of society. It has regarded them as lazy and unwilling to pull themselves up by their own bootstraps. While there are indeed such people, many are excluded from bettering their lives through no fault of their own. The huge unemployment figures that occur when the economy goes sour are not created by people who do not want to work or do not work hard enough. There is also a legacy of racism in this country that does not go away. Discipleship requires an active concern for others. As the Evangelical activist Jim Wallis noted many years ago, the social problem Jesus speaks of most often in the gospels is the problem of rich and poor. No form of discipleship is complete without taking this into mind.

A Church Vocation as a Vehicle for Discipleship

The church is both an institution and a spiritual reality. As an institution it is often the object of distrust in a post-survival society. Some of that distrust is earned. Failures on the part of church leaders and of ordinary churchgoers are frequent enough to make this point. It is flawed, as are all institutions. But it is also a spiritual reality, a communion of believers who are the Body of Christ for the world today. Religion is frequently a motivation for conflict, but much of the peacebuilding in the world today is done by religious bodies as well. A church vocation that at once builds up the Body of Christ and is also the face of the church to the larger world is a vehicle for living out discipleship in a very religious country that is always in need of God's grace and healing. Knowing more about the context in which that discipleship takes place can only make that discipleship more effective. Discipleship does not float above the earth; it is embedded in a concrete time and place.

For Reflection

- To what extent do you recognize yourself and your peers in this description of U.S. culture?
- Which of the challenges of discipleship speak most to your own experience?

Scripture Passages

Matthew 5:13-16	Matthew 6:19-34	Matthew 19:16-30
Mark 8:34-38	John 15:1-17	Ephesians 2:11-22

Recommended Reading

Baker, Wayne. *America's Crisis of Values: Reality and Perception.* Princeton, NJ: Princeton University Press, 2005.

Howe, Neil, and William Strauss. *Millennials Rising: The Next Great Generation.* New York: Vintage, 2000.

Inglehart, Ronald. *Modernization and Postmodernization: Cultural, Economic and Political Change in 43 Societies.* Princeton, NJ: Princeton University Press, 1997.

Norris, Pippa, and Ronald Inglehart. *Sacred and Secular: Religion and Politics Worldwide.* New York: Cambridge University Press, 2004.

Wuthnow, Robert. *After Heaven: Spirituality in America since the 1950s.* Berkeley: University of California Press, 1998.

3

Robin Ryan, CP

The Foundations and Dynamics of Prayer

If you stroll through any popular bookstore you will find a wide array of books on the topic of prayer, written from a variety of religious perspectives. Prayer is a hot topic these days, and it sells lots of books. Some of these publications are helpful while others seem somewhat vague in their approach to praying. One begins to wonder if prayer is only about "mechanics" and about getting in touch with oneself. It seems that Catholic Christians need a more solid foundation for prayer than we sometimes receive from popular writings about it.

In order to discern one's vocation, it is necessary to become a person of prayer. Prayer is the food for our life with God; without it we suffer from malnourishment. For Christians, prayer is much more than mechanics. It is deeply rooted in what we believe about the character of God and the way in which God relates to us. In this chapter, I will first focus on the foundations of prayer. Then I will explore some of the dynamics of prayer, with an eye to principles rather than mechanics. Throughout this exploration of prayer I will draw on the Scriptures as well as the writings of some teachers of prayer in our rich tradition.

The Foundations of Prayer

The Wonder of Grace

What is it that we believe as Christians that gives us the confidence that we can actually talk to God and listen to God? What are the central convictions of our faith that move us to approach prayer with trust and confidence? The most fundamental answer to these questions is our belief in and experience of *grace*. We believe that God is a gracious God. The story of salvation that is cherished by Christians tells us that God has freely chosen to give of self as one to be known and loved. Creation itself is a gift from God. This vast and ancient universe that we inhabit is the good gift of a benevolent God. As Catholic Christians we also affirm that grace is a kind of "second gift" from God. Having created us, God could have (theoretically) remained distant from us. God could have set the universe in motion and simply let it be. But the Bible tells us that this was never the case. The Scriptures teach us that from the very origins of human existence God chose to enter into covenant with women and men. The Bible assures us that God was always acting to draw us into relationship with himself.

One theologian who wrote in compelling ways about the wonder of grace was the German Jesuit Karl Rahner. Rahner emphasized the *interpersonal* character of grace. Grace is not a thing; grace is first and foremost God's self-communication. Grace is God's gift of self as one to be known and loved. Rahner suggested that even though God could have created this world and remained the distant, inaccessible Creator, we can infer from the Scriptures that God's real desire—what was really on God's mind from the very beginning of creation—was God's desire to give of self to us. Rahner proposes that we might think about the deepest desires in the heart of God in this way: "God wishes to communicate himself, to pour forth the love which he himself is. That is the first and last of his real plans and hence of his real world, too. Everything else exists so that this one thing might be: the eternal miracle of infinite love. And so God makes a creature

whom he can love: he creates man. He creates him in such a way
that he *can* receive this Love which is God himself, and that he
can and must at the same time accept it for what it is: the ever-
astonishing wonder, the unexpected, unexacted gift."[1]

Rahner is suggesting that if someone asked us, "What is life
all about, anyway? What does it all mean?" the Christian answer
might well be stated in this way: "There is a God, and this God
wanted to give of self in love." That is the deepest meaning
of reality; it is the "logic" at the heart of the universe. Rahner
emphasizes that God's self-communication is pure gift. Grace is
not earned or demanded. And he reminds us that it is offered to
people who can accept this gift of God's self in freedom. God's
self-communication is not coercive and it is not magic. Grace is
a personal gift that invites a personal response—a response of
the whole person.

Rahner also reminds us that this self-communication of God
is not a reality that remains abstract or ethereal. It is not like
some vapor or ozone layer hanging over us. Rather, God's self-
communication becomes incarnated; it gets enfleshed. Because
human beings are a unity of spirit and flesh, God's gift of self
to us must also become enfleshed. Christians are convinced that
this action of God to give of self in love reached its culmination
in the incarnation of the Son of God—when the Word became
flesh in Jesus Christ. In Christ, God's self-communication became personal in one who entered into our history, who in his
humanity was like us in all things but sin.

It is very important that we begin our exploration of prayer
by reflecting on the gift of grace. Life with God is not like training for a "spiritual triathlon," where if we run enough 10Ks,
swim enough laps in the pool, and practice biking up those hills,
we will have an outstanding showing on the day of the race.
We certainly do need to put forth effort in the practice of our
faith—significant effort. But we must always remember that, at
its heart, our life with God is a *response*. It is a response to God's
faithful, tenacious love for us. This is articulated beautifully in
the First Letter of John: "God's love was revealed among us in
this way: God sent his only Son into the world so that we might

live through him. In this is love, not that we loved God but that he loved us and sent his Son to be the atoning sacrifice for our sins" (1 John 4:9-10). This classic biblical text expresses the heart of the matter: discipleship and everything about the Christian life, including prayer, is a response to the love of God, which was manifested most astoundingly in Jesus Christ.

This self-communication of God is present in a dynamic way in our lives. It has real effects. Through it God is constantly offering us life, light, and love, and God is drawing us toward union with himself. One of the prefaces for the Mass says something that is illuminating for our reflection on prayer: "Our desire to thank you is itself your gift" (Preface for Weekdays IV). When we desire to pray we can be sure that this is an indication that God's grace is already at work within us. Even the yearning to converse with God is already a sign of God's action within us, drawing us closer to himself.

The Call to Friendship with Christ

One way of thinking about the action of grace in our lives is the call to *friendship*. In the Gospel of John, in that section of the gospel known as the farewell discourse, Jesus surprises his disciples with these words: "No one has greater love than this, to lay down one's life for one's friends. You are my friends if you do what I command you. I do not call you servants any longer, because the servant does not know what the master is doing; but I have called you friends, because I have made known to you everything that I have heard from my Father" (John 15:13-15). The disciples are no longer to consider themselves simply as servants, students, or apprentices, but as *friends* of Jesus. In and through Jesus they are being invited into friendship with the God whom he addresses as "Abba" (Father). This is a vitally important moment in the gospel narrative.

We need to remember the context of this farewell discourse in the gospel. It is set within the atmosphere of Jesus' "hour"—the hour of his impending passion and death. Prior to his words to the disciples about friendship, Jesus had told them, "Do not let your hearts be troubled" (John 14:1). But this had to be a very troubling hour for them. They must have been filled with anxiety, wondering what would happen to him and what would happen to them. It is in this charged and tense atmosphere that Jesus calls them his friends. And at this moment he reveals the depths of his friendship-love by proclaiming what he will soon do: "No one has greater love than this, to lay down one's life for one's friends." This will be the defining mark of his friendship with them.

One great teacher of prayer in our tradition who has built on this theme of friendship with Christ is Teresa of Avila, the sixteenth-century Carmelite mystic, reformer, and doctor of the church. Teresa was a woman of tremendous strength, courage, and initiative. For many years she lived a life in religious community that she felt was neither authentic nor satisfying. But when she was thirty-nine years old, she experienced a call to closer communion with Christ. In her autobiography, Teresa offers what may be the most insightful description of prayer ever given. It is set within the context of friendship, echoing what Jesus said to his disciples. Teresa says that in her opinion prayer "*is nothing else than an intimate sharing between friends; it means taking time frequently to be alone with Him who we know loves us.*"[2] This is a very simple description of prayer. At the same time it is a profound insight based on friendship with Christ. Further along in this same work, Teresa writes about gazing on the humanity of Jesus, saying, "*The Lord helps us, strengthens us, and never fails; he is a true friend.*"[3] The Lord Jesus is "true friend." Throughout her autobiography, as Teresa is describing the dynamics of prayer in her own life, she refers to Jesus as true friend at our side. This enduring sense of friendship was central to her prayer and to her journey toward union with God.

Philosophers, theologians, and spiritual writers through the ages have reflected on the defining characteristics of friendship-love. They have taught us that one essential quality of friendship is mutuality, or reciprocity. Paul Wadell, a contemporary moral theologian, puts it this way: "Friendship is mutual or reciprocal love in which each person knows the good they offer another is also the good the other wishes for them. This [second] characteristic of friendship attests that friends are those who recognize each other's love and share it, the exchange of which is the soul of the relationship."[4] If Christ invites us into friendship with himself, there is meant to be a sense of mutuality about this relationship. And this mutuality is at the heart of the dynamics of prayer. Prayer is a dialogue, not a monologue. There is a movement of giving and receiving love in our relationship with Christ. This is what Teresa described so poignantly as "an intimate sharing" with Christ.

Mutuality in our relationship with Christ entails a lot of different things, including simply articulating our love for Christ in a regular, heartfelt way, as one might do in a close relationship with another person. It also means making ourselves vulnerable enough to accept Christ's love for us, allowing him to draw close to us. This may be the place where we struggle the most. Sometimes we draw back in fear or anxiety, aware of our own weakness and sinfulness. We feel unworthy and find it difficult to believe that Christ could really love us. Or it may be that we are afraid of what Christ will ask of us. We may fear that we will not be able to carry it out. In our life with Christ and in our prayer we may try to "do a lot" for Christ, but we may be reticent about simply allowing Christ to draw close to us, to be present to us. But if our friendship with Christ is to deepen and mature, we must allow ourselves to receive from him, as well as give back to him. There should be a genuine reciprocity in our friendship with Christ.

The Dynamics of Prayer

Prayer as Loving Attention

Teresa offered a general description of personal prayer using friendship language—taking time frequently to be alone with Christ, our friend. When we ask what it is that we actually do when we pray, we can borrow again from Karl Rahner, as well as from Bishop Robert Morneau (author of the chapter on discernment in this book). Rahner speaks of prayer in terms of opening our hearts to God. More precisely, he says, "It is not the speaking of many words, or the hypnotic spell of the recited formula; it is the raising of the heart and mind to God in constantly renewed acts of love."[5] Bishop Morneau speaks of the practice of prayer simply as "loving attention."[6] Perhaps we might blend these descriptions and say that when we take time to pray we are *attending with love to God and, in so doing, opening our minds and hearts to God's presence.*

That sounds wonderful, doesn't it? But it is not always as easy as it sounds. It requires a significant amount of self-discipline and practice. How adept are we at attending? How skilled are we in being present to someone in an attentive way? Many of us struggle with being fully present to others or to what we are doing. When someone is talking with us, we have to concentrate and discipline ourselves in order to focus on what the other person is saying and not think about what we have to do next or what just happened five minutes ago. We find it hard to do one thing at a time. "Multitasking" is a term often used these days for the ability to handle a number of things at once. We value people who are proficient at multitasking. But when we pray we are invited to put aside multitasking for a while. We are called to "un-multitask." And this is where we often struggle.

In prayer we are asked to attend to the God who is already present to us—closer to us than we are to ourselves. We do not manufacture God's presence in prayer. And we do not fly off in our "spiritual space shuttle" to the distant planet where God resides. Rather, we consciously attend to the God who holds us in being, who is transcendent yet always near. This is the God whose deepest desire is to give of self to us as one to be known and loved.

There are some things that can help us in this attending. First of all, setting aside a specific time each day for prayer gives us a sacred "space" in our day. It is best to begin with a short period and to build from there. There will certainly be days in which we will not be able to use that time for prayer, but designating a time in which we usually pray helps us to integrate prayer into the rhythm of our lives. Second, we need to find a place that is conducive to quiet and loving attention—a space where we like to be. Third, paying attention to our posture and our breathing can also help us to "tune in." The physical dimensions of prayer are important. Fourth, it often helps us to attend, to center ourselves, by beginning with a passage from Scripture, like the gospel for the Mass of the day or one of the psalms. We can focus on these words, praying them slowly and reflectively, savoring them. Finally, the use of a phrase that is repeated slowly (for example, "Jesus, have mercy on me") can help us to center our minds and hearts on God. When we find ourselves drifting off in distraction, simply repeating that phrase slowly can help us to attend. All of this takes discipline and practice. We may initially shy away from it, as we often do from any activity that requires discipline. But the more we try it, the more natural it becomes and the more we look forward to praying. We find it to be a source of nourishment and refreshment in the midst of life's many demands.

In a marvelous book on prayer based on talks given in Germany soon after the end of World War II, Rahner drew on an experience that must have been imprinted on the minds of the members of the congregation. He referred to their experience of fleeing to air-raid shelters during times in which their city was bombed during the war. After the explosions, they would emerge from the shelters covered with debris. He said, "Let this be taken as the symbol of modern life."[7] Rahner suggested that we often find our hearts to be obstructed, buried under debris. He thinks that this image, though not the most pleasant, often applies to us as we come to prayer. We frequently find our hearts buried beneath all of the debris of life. This "rubble" can consist of many different things: the worries and anxieties that flood our minds; experiences of disappointment and suffering, which can leave us hardened or even embittered; resentments that we harbor because of the way others have treated us; the masks we wear to impress others. Rahner reminds us that when we come to God in prayer we need to ask God to set our hearts free. We must invite God to clear away the rubble that covers our hearts so that we can be free to attend to his presence with love, joy, and openness.

An Attitude of Reverence

What is the tone or atmosphere of prayer? Bishop Morneau suggests that this tone is meant to be one of reverence, wonder, and awe.[8] In an extended meditation on the virtue of reverence, Morneau suggests that it is a virtue that seems to be in rather short supply in our contemporary world. In order to pray well, we must cultivate a stance of reverence toward all of life. Conversely, a vibrant life of prayer deepens our sense of reverence.

I have learned about the meaning of this virtue through the example of other people in my life. A few years ago, I officiated at the wedding of the daughter of some friends. When it came time for the distribution of Communion at the wedding liturgy, I noticed a couple slowly making their way toward me. It was clear that the husband was suffering from severe physical impairment. His wife was gently, carefully helping him up the aisle to receive Communion. At the wedding reception I found myself seated at the table with this couple, who happened to be the aunt and uncle of the bride. During the course of the meal, I discovered that the husband had been a detective in the New York City police department. This tall, strapping man, who had once been in excellent physical condition, had suffered a serious stroke a few years earlier. I watched as his wife lovingly assisted him throughout the meal, helping him with his food and supplying a napkin when it was needed. This wedding reception included a disc jockey who was playing the most popular songs while people danced the night away. At one point he played a song that everyone knew, including the older generation of guests. Almost everyone made their way out to the dance floor to dance to this song. I was left at the table with this couple. The wife told me that, before her husband's stroke, they were always the first couple out on the dance floor and the last to leave. Now, of course, her husband was not able to dance. But I watched as she stood beside her husband's chair at the table, smiled at him, gently took his hand, and moved it up and down to the beat of the music. It was as if they were still dancing—still dancing—even though her husband could no longer make it out to the dance floor.

Observing this couple was a lesson in the virtue of reverence for me. The way in which the wife interacted with her husband and found a way to "dance" with him despite his disability was a radiant example of reverence for another person. Bishop Morneau observes, "Reverence is a power, a grace, and a responsibility. Without reverence, ministry becomes manipulative, Eucharist superficial, and prayer hollow. If the Western world is marked by a growing decline of reverence, the Christian task is clear."[9] Reverence is the virtue that enables us to acknowledge and affirm the dignity of every person. Reverence sends up warning flares when we are tempted to assess people according to how useful they can be to us. As Morneau points out, reverence extends to the way in which we view life in general. It influences the way we look at the gift of time, neither wasting time nor rushing from one thing to the next, from one person to the next. Reverence enables us to recognize particular moments in life that summon us to step back and pay special attention— moments like birth, death, pain, commitment, accomplishment, and loss. Reverence impels us to reflect on our patterns of consumption—to take what we need but not to be greedy or avaricious, as if the whole world belonged to us or our worth were determined by how much we possess. As Morneau suggests, reverence gives birth to hope because it is based on a power greater than us and our own abilities—the power of God.

The virtue of reverence and the practice of prayer go hand in hand. Morneau is right in saying that without reverence our prayer tends to become "hollow." When we pray it is important to remember that we are in the presence of the God who created this immense and mysterious universe. This is the Creator who holds all of life in his hands. This awareness should not make us draw back in fear because, as Jesus tells us, we are invited into friendship with God. But authentic prayer involves transcending our individual worlds to attend to the presence of an awesome God. When we catch a glimpse of God's love for us, this experience leads us into even deeper reverence. This reverence in prayer is meant to color our whole approach to life, to other people, to our use of time and space, and to the very earth that God has given us, which is under such threat today. Reverence is a virtue that is essential to Christian prayer.

The Challenge of Honesty

Accentuating the tone of reverence in prayer does not mean that we should put on a "holy face" when we come before the Lord. Our prayer is always meant to be an expression of our true selves, with all of the light and darkness that is part of our lives. In this regard, Bishop Morneau enunciates an essential principle of prayer: "*In prayer I must bring this me to the living and true God.*"[10] I must bring "this me" to God—not the self I hope to become some day when I have my life in order. Knowing that we can come to the living God as we are is a liberating discovery. It is also an ongoing challenge.

This principle is liberating because it is grounded in our belief in the compassion of God. In prayer we come before the God who knows us through and through and takes us where we are. Time and again, the gospels tell us that when people sincerely sought to encounter Jesus, he accepted them and responded to them. He did not send them away until they got their lives together and were worthy to stand in his presence. The story of the sinful woman in Luke 7 is a classic example of the way in which Jesus related to people who approached him. Jesus is at dinner in the house of Simon the Pharisee when a woman, known in the town as a sinner, slips into the house. Weeping, she bathes the feet of Jesus with her tears and dries them with her hair. She has a deep need and an intense desire to encounter Jesus, despite her sinfulness. Simon concludes that Jesus must not be a prophet because, if he were, he would know who she was and would never let her touch him. Jesus, undaunted by the critical looks he is receiving, reminds the other guests of the humble, loving way in which this woman has approached him. He says to Simon, "You did not anoint my head with oil, but she has anointed my feet with ointment. Therefore, I tell you, her sins, which were many, have been forgiven; hence, she has shown great love" (Luke 7:46-47). Jesus accepts this woman and offers her forgiveness.

Knowing that we can bring our real selves to the living God is tremendously freeing. But it can also be very challenging for us. We may have a self-image that is more negative than positive. The "default mode" of our psyches may be basically negative. Constant criticism by others in our families or among our friends may have instilled a sense of self-loathing within us. We may be haunted by that gut feeling that we will never quite measure up. If that is the case, it is difficult to affirm our inner goodness and accept our personal limitations. So we may find it too risky to share our real selves with anyone, even God. Or we may feel badly about some of the things we have done in the past and are afraid to bring them before God. We assume that we can bring ourselves to the living and true God only after we have taken care of our problems. It may be, too, that we are so accustomed to wearing masks in life that we find it difficult to get in touch with the person we really are. All of us have certain roles to fulfill in our lives, but none of these roles defines the essence of who we are. If our sense of self consists only of the roles we assume, it will be difficult to bring "this me" to the living God.

In order to become a person of prayer, it is essential to speak to the Lord as honestly as we can about what is going on in our lives. The use of set words in prayer is appropriate and can be very helpful. Our Catholic tradition offers us a rich treasury of such prayers, from the psalms to the rosary. But we also need to incorporate into our personal prayer some spontaneous conversation with God. We need to talk with God directly about what we are hoping for and what we may be struggling with. It is important for us to share our joys and accomplishments with God as well as our sadness, disappointments, and confusion. We need to bring to God even those feelings that seem negative to us, like fear, anger, resentment, and jealousy. This kind of honest communication is crucial for discerning one's vocation. Through it we come into deeper touch with ourselves and we allow our entire selves to be present to God.

We can learn about the importance of bringing "this me" to the living God from the Hebrew Scriptures, especially the psalms. The church makes ample use of the psalms in its liturgical prayer. If we peruse the 150 psalms in the Bible we encounter the entire gamut of human emotions—from intense joy and celebration to confusion, anger, and heartrending lamentation. This tells us something important about the Jewish approach to prayer. For the Hebrew people, God was so real to them, such an intimate part of their lives, they knew they could bring anything to God. In fact, they realized that they should bring everything to God in prayer. And in this way God became ever more real to them, ever more a vital part of their lives. The psalms teach us important lessons about bringing "this me" to the living and true God.

This honesty in prayer includes asking for what we need in the concrete circumstances of our lives. Most people know that prayer is about more than just petition. Prayer that only consists of asking God for what we need is impoverished. But we should not go to the other extreme, either—the extreme of denigrating the prayer of petition. In his book on prayer, Karl Rahner writes about people who think that petition represents a "lower" form of prayer that should be left behind in favor of a loftier, more "spiritual" approach to God.[11] These people believe that we should never ask God for our daily bread, healing from sickness, employment, safe travel, or the like. We should only petition God for spiritual goods like patience, purity of heart, courage, the willingness to endure suffering, and so forth.

Rahner concludes that both extremes are wrong—the view that prayer consists only of petition and the idea that we should never ask God to respond to our earthly needs. Prayer is certainly about more than just petition. But, as Rahner points out, "We feel a deep need to turn to God and lift pleading hands of prayer to him."[12] We may never be able to figure out how the prayer of petition "works" through precise theological analysis. Still, Rahner reminds us that the Scriptures teach us to turn to

God for the real, concrete needs of our lives. And he points us to the prayer of Jesus in Gethsemane. In his prayer, Jesus asked that the cup of suffering be removed from him. As Rahner puts it, "It pleased his infinite goodness to let us hear in his words the anguished cry of a man; for he did not ask for something sublime or heavenly, but for that mortal life to which we all cling so tenaciously."[13] At the same time, Jesus exemplified a readiness to accept the will of the Father: "Not my will but yours be done." His prayer in the garden became an offering of his life to the Father. Rahner suggests that these two elements of Jesus' Gethsemane prayer should characterize the prayer of petition in our lives as well. We need to present our real, down-to-earth needs to God in humble prayer. Rahner observes that "a truly Christian prayer of petition is a prayer which is essentially human."[14] At the same time, Jesus teaches us that this asking should be permeated with an attitude of trust in God and acceptance of God's will. God knows and sees things that we cannot know or see. And God always desires what is best for us. Ultimately, the prayer of petition means coming to God with the heart of a child. Rahner says, "To lead a truly Christian life is to place one's whole being into the hands of God as confidently as a child takes the guiding hand of its father."[15]

My oldest brother died of brain cancer a few years ago. He underwent surgery to remove a tumor, but the doctors informed us that the type of cancer from which he was suffering almost always recurs. During the days after his surgery, a close relative expressed her deep confusion and frustration to me about her prayer. She said that in my brother's illness and in some other situations that were important to her it felt as if God was not hearing her prayers. She suggested that, given the diagnosis, perhaps we should not pray for healing for my brother. It might be better simply to pray for the willingness to accept the outcome. I thought long and hard about what she said to me because I too was wrestling with the question of how to pray in this situation. As I did, two insights came to me. First of all, it became clear that we needed to bring our feelings of frustration and of loss directly to God. This was part of our coming to God as we were.

Like the psalmists, it was important for us to lament, even to complain to God. Second, I became convinced that we should pray for healing for my brother, all the while entrusting him to God's care and providence. It was the natural and loving thing to want my brother to be healed of his cancer, even though a physical healing did not appear likely. Not to pray for such a healing would seem inhuman. And we could be sure that God would answer our prayers for healing. That healing might not be a cure from cancer, as it was not in the long run. But it could be a healing for my brother in spirit and mind and the ultimate healing of eternal life. It might also be healing for the family. To come to God as we were at that time, to bring ourselves before the living God, meant bringing our confusing welter of feelings honestly to God and asking God for the gift of healing.

Of all the principles and characteristics of prayer, this is the single most important: to come before God as we are, to bring "this me" to the living and true God. Just as in our human relationships, so too our relationship with God is built and sustained on the foundation of honest communication. We are invited to make our lives, with all of their everyday activities and concerns, an ongoing dialogue with the Lord.

Listening in Prayer

We have explored the invitation to speak to God in prayer. The other dimension of communication with God is, of course, listening. It is important to recall that the dynamics of prayer have their foundation in the reality of God's self-communication. One essential aspect of these dynamics, then, is listening to God and discerning God's self-communication to us.

The listening dimension of prayer is not simple or easy. There is no single, foolproof method for discerning God's word to us, though spiritual masters like Ignatius of Loyola have set forth rules and principles of discernment. As we try to move to an interior quiet and stance of listening in prayer, we usually encounter a whole host of movements and voices at different levels of our being. Some of this inner noise represents the more superficial thoughts, concerns, and desires that are part of our lives. Sometimes we hear within ourselves feelings or tendencies that disturb us, like jealousy and resentment. Listening for God means moving down to our deepest desires, to the very center of our being. It is there that God's desires for us and our own deepest desires intersect. At that still, center point we are able to discern the voice of God. This kind of insight is less the product of logic or strict reasoning, and more the result of intuition, or what Bishop Morneau calls "listening love."[16]

When we listen for God it is not as if we are expecting to hear voices resounding from the walls of the room or through our iPods. But God does have his own mysterious ways of communicating with us. God may speak to us through a Scripture passage that we are reflecting on or that just comes to mind at the right moment. Sometimes we listen to a Scripture passage for the tenth time and it is as if we were hearing it for the first time. It seems to speak directly to a situation or concern that we are facing at that moment. God may speak to us through a sense of interior peace that we experience, perhaps in a time of external turmoil. God sometimes speaks to us simply through a good idea or a sense of direction that we need to follow in our lives. And God certainly speaks to us through the words of other people in our lives, especially those to whom we entrust our hearts.

When I was discerning whether or not to make final profession as a member of the Passionist Congregation and move on to priestly ordination, I spent a lot of time listening in prayer. Part of me was still drawn to marriage and family life, so I was wrestling with this decision. Secretly, I hoped that at some point I would receive a clear, resounding message from God telling me exactly what I should do. Sometimes we wish that God would speak to us in the same clear way as the voice from the GPS that spells out driving directions. I never received that clear, resounding message in prayer. What I did experience was a deepening sense of peace and of "rightness" about the decision to live my life as a Passionist priest. More and more, I felt that I would become my best self by making final commitment as a vowed religious. I sensed that this was the way in which my friendship with Christ would grow and deepen. Such a sense of peace or rightness is often the way in which God communicates with us.

In prayer, then, there are two who are active: the praying person and God. In order to become attuned to the action of God, we need to integrate some time for quiet listening into our prayer. There will be times in which we experience God speaking to us in his own subtle, mysterious ways. On other occasions that time of listening will consist simply of a mutual *presence to*: our presence to God and God's presence to us. It is like two good friends who can enjoy one another's company at dinner without exchanging a lot of words. That quiet presence is itself a marvelous gift.

Rhythms in Prayer

Great teachers of prayer like Teresa of Avila and Paul of the Cross (the founder of the Passionist Congregation) have told us that usually, as one progresses in one's life with God, prayer becomes more simple. While the discipline involved in the early stages of prayer requires more conscious effort and mental activity, those who mature in prayer usually experience it as a quieter, simpler presence to the Lord. They experience less of their own activity and more of God's activity. There is no single, uniform pattern for the way in which this progression takes place in the lives of different people, but it is a general tendency that has been noted by many spiritual masters.

Most people also experience periods in which prayer seems dry and unsatisfying. We may feel that we are not "getting anywhere" in prayer and God may seem very distant from us. We may find it difficult to bring ourselves to prayer. The great spiritual masters tell us that such "desert times" are quite normal. They can actually be periods in which significant spiritual growth takes place. What is essential in such times is to *maintain the communication*—even when it may appear as if little communication is taking place. In close relationships with other people, we usually encounter stages that are difficult or challenging. We know how important it is to keep communicating even during those times. By walking together through those periods, the relationship is strengthened. So too in our relationship with God it is essential to maintain communication even in the desert periods.

Finally, as many spiritual writers point out, while there are basic principles and guidelines for prayer that are helpful for everyone, there is no single, uniform way to pray. Teresa of Avila wrote that God does not lead all by the same road. Different people are drawn to different types of prayer for a variety of reasons: their upbringing in the faith, personality, and formative experiences in their lives. So a certain pluralism in prayer is normal and desirable. The most important thing is that we actually enter into prayer with a spirit of dedication and faithfulness.

Conclusion

I began this reflection on prayer by speaking about God's gracious gift of self to us and the way in which Christ invites each of us into a relationship of friendship. While the call to become a person of prayer presents real challenges to us and requires genuine commitment, it is ultimately a profound gift. The more we pray the more prayer becomes the nourishment of our souls. Progress in prayer is really about growing in the realization that we are loved by God in a way that exceeds our wildest imaginings. We are summoned to come to a deeper, more personal knowledge of God in order that we may receive God's love and share it with others.

For Reflection

- Who are the people in your life who have been examples of prayer for you? What did you learn from them?
- What are the important characteristics of your relationship with your closest friends? How might these qualities apply to your relationship with Christ?
- What do you find to be most rewarding about prayer? What is most challenging?

Scripture Passages

Psalm 63	Psalm 121	Luke 7:36-50
Luke 11:1-13	Ephesians 3:14-21	1 John 4:7-21

Recommended Reading

Green, Thomas. *Opening to God: A Guide to Prayer*. Notre Dame, IN: Ave Maria Press, 1977.

Merton, Thomas. *New Seeds of Contemplation*. New York: New Directions Books, 1961.

Morneau, Robert. *Spiritual Direction: Principles and Practices*. New York: Crossroad, 1996.

Rahner, Karl. *On Prayer*. Collegeville, MN: Liturgical Press, 1993.

4

Bishop Robert Morneau

The Art of Discernment

Discernment is a grace. It is the art of recognizing God's voice and responding to God's call with our whole being. Implicit in this art is a listening heart and a passion to do God's will. In his masterful book *Asking the Fathers*, Aelred Squire presents discernment's mission statement somewhat in these terms: to respond to the spiritual fullness of each moment. The grace of discernment is necessary to achieve this spiritual goal.

For the past several years I have had the privilege of participating in a five-day conference at the Catholic Theological Union. Under the leadership of Fr. Robin Ryan and funded by the Lilly Endowment, young adults come together to ponder and pray over their personal journeys and what God might be calling them to be and do. Catholics on Call has been a transformative experience for many of the participants as they reflect upon presentations, share common prayer, experience a variety of ministerial activities, and enjoy the building of community through meals and leisure time. My assignment was to speak about the process of discernment both in theory and in practice.

This essay will deal with discernment in a threefold manner. First, I will discuss the way in which discernment is grounded in the sacrament of baptism, our initiation into the life of Christ.

Second, I offer ten principles of discernment that I have found to be meaningful in both giving and receiving spiritual direction. These principles were originally published in my 1992 book *Spiritual Direction: A Path to Spiritual Maturity* (New York: The Crossroad Publishing Company, no longer in print). Third, I offer several writers—poets, mystics, novelists, essayists, theologians, and philosophers—who have served as mentors on my journey. I am indebted to them and will present the insights they have so generously shared.

Baptismal Call(s)

Discernment is directly related to baptism, our entrance into the life of Jesus and the Christian community. In that sacrament, later to be strengthened in confirmation and nourished by the Eucharist, five calls are given: the call to maturity, the call to holiness, the call to community, the call to service, and the call to generosity. Thus, before discerning that one should marry, be single, be ordained or consecrated to religious life, the fundamental vocation(s) is that of responding to the five calls of baptism. Everyone has to work out a double discernment as a disciple of Christ Jesus.

Discerning Maturity

How are we to assess our spiritual growth? Dag Hammarskjöld (1905–61), former secretary general of the United Nations, raised this question in his journal *Markings*: "Do we ever grow up?" When Jesus was found in the temple by Mary and Joseph and headed back home, we are told that he grew in age and wisdom and in the favor of God (Luke 2:40). We are all in the process of "becoming." Whether we are growing in love and knowledge is a crucial discernment question.

James and Evelyn Whitehead, a pastoral theologian and developmental psychologist, respectively, offer three criteria for discerning maturity: discipleship, charity, and stewardship.[1]

If we are developing an ever deeper sense of our identity and destiny, if we are nurturing our ability to care and love, if we are good stewards of all God's gifts, then we have certitude that the seeds of God's grace are developing and, in all likelihood, bearing much fruit. Perhaps we never totally grow up but we are called to ongoing spiritual ripeness.

Discerning Holiness

Within the Catholic tradition, holiness is essentially "the perfection of love." When we celebrate the feast of Saint Thérèse of Lisieux (1873–97) on October 1, we are reminded that she discerned her vocation to be that of love. More specifically, she felt called "to make Love loved." In other words, her vocation was that of holiness and she would have nothing of being "half" a saint. She longed for the fullness of God's grace and she longed to share that grace with the world. In 1997, Pope John Paul II declared Thérèse a Doctor of the Church, holding up to the world a person who discerned and lived God's calling. Anyone interested in watching the discernment process unfold would benefit from reading Thérèse's *Story of a Soul.*

Sanctity and holiness may seem to be out of reach for most of us. Too much is demanded; too many sacrifices have to be made. Again, Saint Thérèse offers her insight. The "little way" of perfection and holiness is to do everything—be it the laundry, a visit to the hospital, cooking a meal, relating to others—in the presence and love of God. Holiness is as simple and as difficult as that. Holiness is to live in the light of God's love, before his face. On my own journey I attempted to capture this call to holiness in the following verse:

On the Log by the River in the Morning

I'm here again.

We sit on the log
watching the river pass by
in the early hours of the morning.

Much darkness floats by:
broken hearts,
troubled minds,
fearful hands.
Yet above the river an ocean of light.

Beside me is the Master.
I do not see him
only feel his presence,
sure and strong.
We talk of yesterday's events,
we plan for today.
All this on the log
by the river
in the morning.

I shall return come nightfall,
as a soldier to his general,
to file my done duties.
Then I shall sleep beside the river
and await our morning conversation.

Discerning Community

One characteristic of our culture is individualism. There is an abiding tendency to take care of oneself to the exclusion of others. "I'm number one" rings out loud and clear. A sense of the common good is weak. The theme of the Mystical Body of Christ, wherein we recognize and try to live the reality that we all are members of Jesus' body, is not ingrained in our religious imagination. A sense of caring and sharing is a core ingredient of our baptismal call. As someone once said, we don't go to heaven alone.

At this level of discernment we turn to the mystery of the Trinity. Here we have a community of persons who live caring and sharing to perfection. God is Love, the Scriptures tell us, and love is all about that "unity" in comm*unity*. As we celebrate the sacraments and ponder God's word, the focus is always on union with God and unity among ourselves. We are made for this oneness; separation is hell. *Thus a foundational standard for discernment is the question of whether or not a thought, an attitude, a behavior leads to union.*

In his challenging book *Call to Conversion*, Jim Wallis holds that it is in community that we open ourselves to genuine conversion. Even more, it is precisely by remaining in a corporate environment that the ongoing process of conversion is preserved and nurtured.[2] We need one another if our minds and hearts are to be truly Christian. It is in community that we are affirmed and challenged, supported and confronted. Discernment doesn't happen in isolation though it does involve some solitude. God gives us one another so that together we might advance in the way of his kingdom.

Discerning Service

Jesus made it clear to his disciples that his was a life of service. This "being-for" others was the Lord's lifestyle. Service or ministry essentially involves two reciprocal elements: identifying needs and naming our gifts. Be that gift one of teaching or healing, of administration or parenting, it becomes both a privilege and a responsibility. And we must be aware of the reciprocal nature of ministry: those who serve are also being served by the ones who are the apparent recipients. Ask any spiritual director and he or she will say they are never sure who is being directed in any given session. Often God speaks to the "server" through the words and life of the one served.

The challenge in this fourth baptismal call is to identify our gifts. Years ago a preacher said: "You can identify your gift by asking the question: *when are you happiest and most alive?* This will give you a good sense of what your gift might be." That same preacher added a footnote: *"Don't stay out of your gifted area too long. It could prove deadly."* Some individuals are most alive in the kitchen preparing a meal. Others are in their most "alive" zone when tending to the sick, plowing a field, enacting legislation, administering a school, telling stories, writing a poem, giving a tour of a cathedral. Saint Paul is eloquent in reminding us that there are so many different gifts but the same Lord and the same Spirit.

Discerning Generosity

Frugality has its proponents. But given the fact that we are made in the image and likeness of an extravagant, generous God, a frugal lifestyle just will not do. Nor will you see much joy or peace in a Silas Marner, the lonely and miserly linen-weaver in George Eliot's novel *Silas Marner*, or in any other penny-pincher. Generosity is the Christian way of life flowing out of a sense of being gifted and grounded in an attitude of gratitude. All is gift; we can claim nothing as ultimately our own. "It's mine" is a lie that too many believe. Our time, our talent, and our treasure come our way to be shared with others.

Discernment leads us to recognize that God wants us to be not only recipients of his blessings but also transmitters of his grace. Thus we are to be stewards, conduits, instruments of the gifts given to us. Hoarding is a deadly art; greed will slay the spirit. The proposition that joy is only possible if a person is a giver can easily be defended. Old Scrooge models for us a joyless life. His failure in generosity is an icon of how not to live. How much time or talent we share, how much money we will give to worthy causes, will be determined by the circumstances of our lives and by the quality of our spiritual life.

The Art of Discernment: Ten Guiding Principles

1. Discernment is a prayerful process whereby experiences are interpreted in faith.

In *Mother Teresa, Come Be My Light: The Private Writings of the "Saint of Calcutta,"* we witness the intense process of discernment Mother Teresa was engaged in. In leaving her religious community to start a new one (1948), she prayed, sought the guidance of her confessor and bishop, and constantly questioned whether she was doing the right thing. One can feel the anguish of her discernment process. In one letter, Mother Teresa writes: "Yet the 'Voice' kept pleading, *'Come, come, carry me into the holes of the poor. Come, be My light.'*"[3] It was in prayer and through the lens of faith that the Saint of Calcutta figured out what God was asking of her.

Experiences, if they are not to dehumanize, must be reflected upon and interpreted. It is possible that even a good experience—a delicious meal, an excellent movie, a stirring liturgy—can makes us less human if we do not take the time to process it. What often happens is that we go from one experience to another without appreciating its value. This is the proverbial rat race. When we stop to reflect and assimilate we enter the land of hermeneutics, the science of interpretation. This is a very complex and involved terrain. Our experiences are multidimensional; our interpretative skills are limited by our training and culture. Yet we have no choice but to step back, invoke the Holy Spirit to fill us with wisdom and insight, and then, after due diligence, respond in deed or word. A faith perspective means that we truly believe that God is operative in the stirrings and whispers of the heart. Faith also convinces us that God will help us align our will with his.

2. Discernment must deal with many voices seeking to capture our minds, hearts, and energy.

How can one hear the voice of God amid the many other "calls" that daily impinge upon our minds and hearts? The number of channels on radio and television, the number of e-mails and phone messages, the number of appointments and invitations so often confuse us and divide our limited energy and wandering attention. The challenge in discernment is to sort out which of these voices are congruent with God's will and which are not. Once done, then we are to respond without hesitation.

If the squeaking wheel gets the grease, the loudest voice tends to get the most attention. Discernment is a means of not allowing this to happen. Noises and repeated messages must be screened out and in prayerful silence we need to listen attentively to the divine call. It may well come through a friend or counselor, through an historical event or illness, but it will not be found in the messages of a decadent culture. Selective viewing of television/movies and selective reading are important practices lest our souls and our hearts become hardened.

3. Discernment is cultivated in a listening love that allows one to hear the felt-experience of good and evil movements within oneself, others, and society.

The Carmelite poet Jessica Powers writes that anyone who lives in the Spirit of God is a listener and a lover. From experience, we all know that neither the art of listening nor the art of loving is easy. Though God's grace is offered, at times we lack openness to these blessings or fail in exercising the discipline needed to lead a listening, loving lifestyle. Our task is cultivation. By striving to be more sensitive to the inner movements of our beings, by making every effort to respond with care to what God asks, we will grow into mature disciples.

One can sense in reading Dag Hammarskjöld's personal journal, *Markings,* that one is in the presence of someone who worked diligently at being sensitive to both the inner movements of his own being, as well as what was happening between and among nations. As the secretary general of the United Nations, Hammarskjöld had tremendous responsibilities as well as great status among world leaders and the general public. Yet, he strove to be true to what he was being asked to do. His life, as reflected in his journal, was one of constant discernment, deep listening.

4. Discernment relies on two foundations: Jesus and revelation.

We need a standard to evaluate the quality of an attitude or action. In the process of discernment, we need some criteria that indicate that we are on the right path. The life of Jesus and the word of God are two such criteria. If a decision or inner movement is harmonious with the ethics and sensibility of Jesus, then we have assurance that God's grace is operative. If what we say or do is congruent with the Scriptures, again there is a strong degree of certainty that we are being faithful to our inmost nature. Thus, the more we know and love the Lord, the more we are conversant with God's word, the better chance we have of doing God's will and building the kingdom. Theologian Gerald O'Collins offers this insight: "This letter [the First Letter of John] proceeds to spell out the two basic criteria (faith in the person of Jesus and effective love for others) which make it possible to discern the spiritual experience that brings authentic communion with God."[4]

The influential Russian novelist Leo Tolstoy (1828–1910) was haunted by the meaning of life, and after an early life of self-indulgence and empty distractions studied the gospel, especially the Sermon on the Mount. Tolstoy came to the conviction that the kingdom of God was within each soul. He preached a life of nonviolence and, when appropriate, civil disobedience. His writings influenced Gandhi and Thoreau as well as thousands of others. Two standards influenced Tolstoy's approach to life: the person of Jesus and the Sacred Scriptures.

5. Discernment assumes that God is continually working in the depth of every individual and community.

God's creative, redeeming, and sanctifying activities are always at work. We live in a *divine milieu*. We can assume that every hour of every day, God's initiatives and interventions are present in our individual lives and among the nations. What we need are antennae to pick up the signals sent our way and to respond with commitment to the divine design. Jeremiah the prophet writes, "For surely I know the plans I have for you, says the Lord, plans for your welfare and not for harm, to give you a future with hope" (Jer 29:11).

Jesus tells us that his Father is always at work (John 5:17). That work is building the kingdom wherein righteousness and peace and joy govern our minds and hearts (Rom 14:17). Saint Francis of Assisi felt deep within the stirring of God's call to rebuild the church. His positive response to the working of God has helped transform our world. Discernment is the ability to perceive God's work and to respond to it with enthusiasm and joy.

6. Discernment respects the nature of time and is willing to wait freely for a decision that needs clarification, detachment, and magnanimity.

Thomas Merton once said that "hurry ruins saints as well as artists."[5] Although a case might be made to act quickly, that imperative follows prayerful deliberation. We should *act on our clarities* but to arrive at this state can take considerable time. Further, our freedom must confront our addictive nature. Until we arrive at a graced detachment from our will in order to do God's will, our judgment is often impaired. Another characteristic of discernment is largeness of soul. Spiritual maturity, like that of nature, often involves years of small, specific acts of renunciation that enlarge our souls and make them open to whatever the Lord might ask. Clarification, detachment, and magnanimity take time. No haste here; no hurry lest it ruin God's precious work.

While appreciating the nature of time and the need for some clarity, there is the possibility of being too patient. Procrastination can infiltrate the soul and keep us from doing things that should obviously be done or induce us to continue to do what should be avoided. Augustine's *Confessions* is a classic in this regard as the great saint tells us how he begged the Lord for continence "but not yet." Procrastination is a desecration of time; procrastination is an alibi for hanging on to what we want.

7. Discernment is a gift (grace) given to those who are properly disposed to receive it because of obedience and surrender.

What enabled Mary, the Mother of Jesus, to give her consent to the angel Gabriel? How was it that Abraham, on that fateful mountain, was able to surrender his most prized possession? What drew Gandhi into a life of nonviolence that helped his people gain liberation? And Saint Francis of Assisi, what grace was operative in his heart as he fell in love with lady poverty and gave everything to the Lord? Two gifts help explain the answer. All of these individuals were obedient; they listened to the voice of the Lord. All of these individuals were willing to surrender their thoughts and ways to what the Lord desired. Of course, at the head of the list is Jesus, who was obedient, obedient even to surrendering to death on the cross (Phil 2:8).

Isaiah the prophet reminds us that our thoughts and our ways are often far distant from the thoughts and ways of the Lord (Isa 55:8). Obedience and surrender are extremely difficult in a culture where self-determination is a prized value. "I did it my way" rings out loud and clear. C. S. Lewis maintained that there are only two types of individuals: those who do God's will and those who do their own. Discernment is a grace; so too are obedience and surrender.

8. Discernment blends faith and pragmatism: it searches out God's will in radical trust and does it.

At the core of William James's philosophy of pragmatism is the conviction that "the true is what works well." While truth is something much more refined than this, truth does work in bringing us into a life of discipleship. Saint James is clear in reminding us that faith is dead without good works (Jas 2:17). In faith we are gifted with a relationship with God and, trusting in divine help, we make decisions that further the growth of God's kingdom. Discipleship is hard work; discipleship demands sacrifice. Saint Paul models for us a pragmatic person of deep faith: he did the truth in love. Such is the call of every follower of Christ.

"Don't talk of love, show me!" This lyric from *My Fair Lady* captures the blending of faith and pragmatism. When love is authentic, action is demanded. The loving person responds with active concern for the beloved. The first and greatest commandment impels us to reach out to those who are in need. The Good Samaritan exemplifies the discerning, loving heart. He saw the victim and offered assistance in a sacrificial fashion. The follower of Jesus is asked to discern life in a similar way.

9. Discernment looks to consequences for its authenticity: decisions are of God if ultimately they lead to life and love.

Saint Paul gives us the classical signs of the presence of God's Spirit and thus the authentic signs of graced discernment. In his letter to the Galatians Paul enumerates those qualities of the working of grace: love, peace, joy, patience, goodness, kindness, trustworthiness, gentleness, and self-control (Gal 5:22). When our choices give evidence of these characteristics, we have considerable assurance that we are on the road to the kingdom. When the lawyer Atticus Finch in Harper Lee's classic *To Kill a Mockingbird* defends an African American who has been unjustly accused of a crime, he gives us an example of a courageous man being an agent of God's life and love although there is no chance of winning the case.

Initially, decisions may appear to be antilife, even antilove. The decision to proceed with a family intervention in the case of alcoholism may be very disrupting, causing members of the family to walk away in bitterness. Yet, after thoughtful prayer, this may be the best thing to do, indeed, the necessary thing to do. Life is complicated; decisions are messy. All that is expected is that one be as responsible and as prayerful as possible and then act. With God's help, there will be an increase of life and love.

10. *Discernment leads to truth and, through truth, into freedom.*
Jesus proclaims that "the truth will make you free" (John 8:32b). A central goal of the spiritual life is to be free, free from all the obstacles that prevent us from doing the will of God. But that freedom is impossible without living in the truth— the truth of God's love, the truth of our sinfulness, the truth of our salvation in Jesus. In an age of agnosticism and rampant skepticism, the possibility of attaining truth has been obscured and, in some cases, denied. But both faith and reason are gateways into reality, the truth of things, be they thick or thin. The art of discernment cuts through false theories and dead-end philosophies to point us to the light. Discernment is grounded in the enlightenment of the Holy Spirit, the Spirit who opens our minds to the truth and empowers our wills to freely do the good.

The southern Catholic writer Walker Percy, in his *The Second Coming*, reminds us that if we listen carefully and with an open mind, truth may arise from unlikely sources. Then he lists them: "from an enemy, from a stranger, from children, from nuts, from overheard conversations, from stupid preachers (certainly not from eloquent preachers!)."[6] Good advice here. In discerning what our vocation is and where the truth of God resides, the Lord will often use surprising avenues to catch our attention. We need but ask Saint Augustine who heard a child's voice cry out.[7] The great Augustine heeded that voice and took another step closer to doing God's will.

Mentors of Discernment

Poets: Robert Frost, Emily Dickinson, George Herbert

Robert Frost's "The Road Not Taken" is a classic example of the discernment process. The poet takes us into the forest where two roads are going off in different directions. Which one to choose? The road well worn by previous pilgrims or the road less traveled by? The traveler in the poem took the less traveled path and that choice made all the difference. *Major moments of discernment are those crossroad experiences that shape our destinies and deeply impact those with whom we travel.*

In her "If I can stop one heart from breaking . . . ," Emily Dickinson presents her standard for meaning. If our choices are those of service, healing broken hearts or helping fallen birds or consoling the suffering, our lives will not be empty or "lived in vain." Though not a great poem, this verse takes us to the heart of the gospel wherein Jesus' mission is one of service. *When our daily decisions are focused on the needs of others and not concentrated on our own well-being, the grace of authentic discernment is operative in our soul.*

The great poet/priest George Herbert is a master mentor in the field of spiritual direction. Three of his greatest poems—"Matins," "Love III," and "Trinity Sunday"—are not only poems but rich prayers. Herbert's last stanza in "Matins" provides enough material for a whole retreat:

> Teach me thy love to know;
> That this new light, which now I see,
> May both the work and workman show:
> Then by a sunbeam I will climb to thee.

In many of his poems, the poet addresses God—a creating, re-deeming, sanctifying God—whose love for us is the central faith fact of our lives. Herbert expresses in verse his own discernment process, giving us the fruits of communication with God. *Discernment attunes us to God's communication and calls us to be both contemplative and apostolic.*

Mystics: Teresa of Avila, John Cassian, Augustine

In her autobiography, Saint Teresa of Avila (1515–82) observes that we can so easily deceive ourselves in our understanding of life and our relationship with God. Two things counter that deception: true humility and the gift of discernment. If these graces are present we will have the ability to judge the spiritual movements in our lives by three things: their fruits, their resolutions, and their love. The essential fruits of the Holy Spirit are love, joy, and peace. If our resolutions lead to a deeper union with God and unity among ourselves, there is no cause to fear deception. And as always, love is the ultimate criterion for discernment for love takes us into the heart of God where all deception and delusions are exposed. *Discernment must be grounded in love and manifested by firm resolutions and good fruits.*

John Cassian, a Christian writer of the early church, warns that we can easily drift off the royal road of discipleship by veering to the right through "stupid presumption and excessive fervor" or veering off to the left through "carelessness and sin."[8] Thus the importance of having some source of objectivity, be it an experienced guide or the teaching of the Bible or the magisterium of the church, to hold up the truth of things. *Discernment is vulnerable to subjectivity.*

"Man's hairs are easier to count than his affections and the movements of his heart." Thus writes the great Augustine. Not only are the whispers, stirrings, hunches, intimations, leadings, nudges, proddings, drawings of the heart numerous, they often contradict one another and pull us in directions that can lead to life or death. Augustine cries out toward the end of the *Confessions* that his love for God was late, oh, so late. "Late have I loved you, beauty, so old and so new: late have I loved you."[9] *The grace of discernment is given so that we might love the Lord now.*

Literature: C. S. Lewis, James Joyce, George Eliot

The Magician's Nephew is one of seven volumes in C. S. Lewis's *The Chronicles of Narnia*. In that work, reference is made to a memory that stayed with Peter, Susan, Edmund, and Lucy Pevensie, the four children in these *Chronicles*, their whole lives. It was the memory of the lion Aslan, the Christ figure, whose golden goodness gave them the assurance that no matter what, everything would be well in the end. That experience of Aslan helped the children deal with fear and sadness, for Aslan was always at hand, "just round some corner or just behind some door." This golden goodness became a reference point by which to evaluate every relationship, attitude, or behavior. *In a discerning heart, God's presence becomes the discerning center for assessing one's entire life.*

In *A Portrait of the Artist as a Young Man*, James Joyce suggests two truths about discernment. First, he uses the Latin phrase *non serviam* (I will not serve) to describe the reaction of a young man, Stephen Dedalus, who attended a school retreat in which the theme of "fire and brimstone" filled the conferences. Upon hearing of this wrathful God, the young man resolved not to serve such a deity. This is an example of "negative" discernment. What was heard did not ring true. Moreover, it was revolting and caused a revolution in the young man's heart. Second, in this semiautobiographical novel Joyce records how young Dedalus rejected the voices of his parents, teachers, classmates, nation, and the profane world and, instead, embarked on his own into a life of art. In the end, this discernment led to the doing of his own will, not that of God. *Discernment has the difficult task of sorting out many voices and this process involves the risk of making wrong decisions.*

In her powerful novel *Adam Bede,* George Eliot describes the anguish that Dinah underwent as she attempted to discern whether to marry or continue in her life of service. Her love for her suitor was strong, but stronger was an awareness of Jesus, the Man of Sorrows, who turned her gaze to the sinful, suffering, and afflicted. Dinah tells Adam, "All my peace and my joy have come from having no life of my own, no wants, no wishes for myself, and living only in God and those of his creatures whose sorrows and joys he has given me to know."[10] Throughout history, individuals have experienced the tug between a life of sacrificial service and living a life committed to another individual and a family. Both demand sacrifices of a different sort. *Discernment demands brutal honesty as well as a sacrificial spirit.*

Theology / Philosophy:
John Shea, Thomas Green, Gerald May, Yves Congar

According to John Shea in his *Stories of God,* God's active presence in our lives can be discerned by a "putting together" rather than a "tearing apart." The terms he uses are "diabolic" and "symbolic," the first referring to fragmentation and the second to integration. He is speaking of behaviors, attitudes, and situations of transition in the lives of people and in the events of history. This criterion fits in well with the biblical emphasis on union and unity in contrast to division and separation. *Discernment assists us in evaluating situations that lead to reconciliation and those that lead to alienation.*

The Jesuit spiritual writer Thomas Green, in his *Darkness in the Marketplace,* reminds us that life is a warfare involving a fierce struggle between good and evil. Discernment is one weapon we have to combat evil movements. Fr. Green recalls that there is a "cardinal principle of discernment that the devil always seeks to enter as an angel of light."[11] What is evil has the appearance of good; what sounds like the voice of God can be a counterfeit calling. *Discernment demands a shrewdness that implies considerable experience of the negative forces of life.*

The art of discernment is not a solitary matter. Often, because of the complexity of situations, our own blind spots, and lack of experience, we need the assistance of individuals trained in the spiritual life for guidance. Gerald May, MD, in his *Care of Mind, Care of Spirit*, offers wise advice in encouraging those who seek to respond to "felt callings, leadings, and inclinations." That advice is twofold: serious prayer and spiritual direction. Fortunately, there is a large corpus of spiritual literature that can help us, in addition to the guidance of a personal spiritual director. The great Quaker writer, Douglas Steere, confirms this need for help in stating that so many hunches and intimations need clarification as well as confirmation. "Hence the call for help."

One of the greatest mentors in the ways of the Holy Spirit is Yves Cardinal Congar. His major work, *I Believe in the Holy Spirit*, is a masterful account of the church's tradition regarding a theology of the Spirit. In speaking of charismatic discernment as a powerful source of knowledge aiding people in their pastoral ministry, Congar quotes the words of another spiritual writer: "The end in view is his [God's] people's freedom from influences which do not come from God and which are replaced by the lordship of Jesus as restored by the Holy Spirit."[12] There are so many influences in our culture that distract us from God's reign, be they individualism, consumerism, or radical narcissism. *Discernment is essentially the work of the Holy Spirit freeing us to be responsive disciples of Jesus.*

Conclusion

Giving the last word to a Doctor of the Church and one who sought God's will beyond anything else is a fitting way to bring these reflections to an end. Saint Thérèse of Lisieux left behind the story of her soul for all to read. It was a story of the "advances of Our Lord" and the deep desire to give all to God. Discernment is all about doing God's will by responding to the hourly "advances" and leadings of the Lord. Here is Thérèse's summary of her whole life:

This little incident of my childhood is a summary of my whole life; later on when perfection was set before me, I understood that to become a saint one had to suffer much, seek out always the most perfect thing to do, and forget self. I understood, too, there were many degrees of perfection and each soul was free to respond to the advances of Our Lord, to do little or much for Him, in a word, to choose among the sacrifices He was asking. Then, as in the days of childhood, I cried out: "My God, I choose all!" I don't want to be a saint by halves, I'm not afraid to suffer for you, I fear only one thing: to keep my own will; so take it, for "I choose all" that You will![13]

For Reflection

• What have been the crossroad experiences that have shaped who I am today?
• Who are the people who have helped me discern God's will? What did I learn from them?
• What are the "noises" in my life that hinder me from hearing the voice of the Lord?
• When am I happiest and most alive? What are my areas of giftedness?

Scripture Passages

Psalm 25	Isaiah 55:6-11	1 Corinthians 12
Galatians 5:22-26	Philippians 2:5-11	James 2:14-26

Recommended Reading

Augustine of Hippo. *Confessions.* Translated by Henry Chadwick. Oxford: Oxford University Press, 1991.
Hammarskjöld, Dag. *Markings.* Translated by Leif Siöberg and W. H. Auden. New York: Knopf, 1965.

Percy, Walker. *The Second Coming*. New York: Farrar, Straus, Giroux, 1980.

Teresa of Avila. *The Book of Her Life: The Collected Works of Teresa of Avila*. Translated by Kieran Kavanaugh and Otilio Rodriguez. Washington, DC: ICS Publications, 1976.

Thérèse of Lisieux. *Story of a Soul: The Autobiography of Thérèse of Lisieux*. Translated by John Clarke. Washington, DC: ICS Publications, 1975.

Wallis, Jim. *Call to Conversion*. New York: Harper & Row, 1981.

5

Thomas P. Rausch, SJ

The Communion of the Church

While the Catholic Church has some obvious institutional aspects, Catholicism itself is an essentially communal expression of Christian faith. It is as far from the contemporary "I'm spiritual but not religious" claim of many today as it is from the individualistic reduction of faith to a personal relationship with Jesus too often characteristic of more conservative American Protestantism.

If being a Christian is to be a member of the church, so also the church is more than the local congregation; the church itself is a global community, a communion of churches. To explore the nature of the communion of the church we will begin first with the movement of Jesus and his disciples. Then we will consider the primitive church in the New Testament, the emergence of the Catholic Church, and three great turning points in the latter church's history.

The Jesus Movement

There were a number of distinct movements in the Judaism of Jesus' time. The Essenes, the descendants of the Hasidim or "righteous ones" who had broken with the Hasmoneans over their usurpation of the priestly office after the Maccabean revolt (165 BCE), are known to history from their community at the Wadi Qumran. They left us the Dead Sea Scrolls. Another movement grew up around John the Baptist; it apparently lasted into early Christian times (Acts 18:24-25). Jesus seems to have been a part of John's group before his own ministry began (see John 3:26). But at some point he separated from John and began to gather his own disciples around him.

From the beginning the disciples of Jesus were different from those of the Pharisees; their role was not just to learn his teachings, but to be in his company (Mark 3:14) and to engage with him in the practices that show forth the reign of God—preaching, healing, and reconciling (Mark 6:7-13; Luke 10:1-10; cf. Rom 14:17).[1] Jesus described his movement as a family, based not on blood or kinship or patriarchy (Luke 14:26) but on obedience to God: "Whoever does the will of God is my brother and sister and mother" (Mark 3:35). The fact that Jesus "made" or "appointed" twelve (Mark 3:14) at the heart of his movement is also significant. Symbolizing the twelve tribes of Israel, it is evidence that Jesus saw his movement as essentially communal, as a new or restored Israel.

The church exists from the time the scattered disciples of Jesus began to reassemble at the news of his resurrection. While Jesus did not "found" the church in the sense of giving it a constitution, ecclesial elements such as the leadership of "the twelve," the central place of Peter, and the rites of baptism and the Eucharist come from Jesus himself. Thus, there are "continuities of belief, personnel, and practice between the group gathered around Jesus in his earthly ministry (the disciples) and the group gathered around the risen Lord (the church)."[2]

The Church in the New Testament

The Greek word *ekklēsia*, originally a secular term, meant those "called out," thus assembly or gathering. It was used in the

Septuagint (the Greek translation of the Hebrew Scriptures) to translate the expression *kehal Yahweh* or "assembly of the Lord" (cf. Num 16:3; Deut 23:2). The New Testament authors used this term for the assembly of the disciples of Jesus; the English word is "church." The New Testament church consisted of a variety of diverse communities—Jewish Christian, Hellenistic, Pauline, and Johannine—spread from Jerusalem to Rome but living in "communion" (*koinōnia*) with each other. As these early communities shared letters from apostolic figures, three root ecclesial metaphors developed—People of God, Body of Christ, and the dwelling place or temple of the Spirit.

People of God

To speak of the church as the People of God is to emphasize the continuity between God's people, Israel, in the Old Testament and the community of the disciples of Jesus. Though the metaphor is used of the Christian community explicitly only once (1 Pet 2:10), the idea that the earliest Christians—all Jews—represented the renewed or eschatological Israel runs throughout the New Testament. It can be found in Paul's letters (1 Cor 10:1-5; Gal 3:6-9; 6:16; and Rom 9–11), in the first letter of Peter (1 Pet 2:10), and in the letter to the Hebrews. The letter to the Hebrews parallels Israel as the people of God with the church as the new people, and it speaks of Christ as the new high priest who has expiated sin by his once-for-all sacrifice and established a new covenant (Heb 8–10).

But it took several generations to grasp the full implications of the revelation of God's love in Christ. Paul's letters and the Acts of the Apostles show the early Christians struggling with the question of the observance of the Jewish law, while Matthew depicts Jesus as the new Moses. Some negative language toward the Pharisees (Matthew) or "the Jews" (John) reflects conflicts between the Christian and Jewish communities in the mid-80s when the Christian Jews were being put out of the synagogue (see John 9:22). So the break between Christianity and Judaism, between 85 and 130, happened relatively late.

Body of Christ

Perhaps Paul's most powerful metaphor for the church is Body of Christ. It first appears in the early 50s in his first letter to the Corinthians. He uses it to show the Corinthians that their community, troubled by internal divisions, was united by baptism (1 Cor 12:13; cf. Gal 3:27-28) and the Lord's Supper (1 Cor 10:16-17) into one body, the Body of Christ. In Colossians and Ephesians, later letters in the Pauline tradition, the Body of Christ has become a metaphor for the whole church, with Christ as its head (Col 1:18; Eph 5:23). In more contemporary terms, our bodies relate us to the world and to other people, making our spirits visible. Without our bodies, we are literally nowhere. So too, the Body of Christ mediates Christ's presence to the world. For Paul the unity of the church as the Body of Christ is rooted in what the later church would call the sacraments of baptism and Eucharist. In the words of Pope Benedict XVI, "The Church is the celebration of the Eucharist; the Eucharist is the Church,"[3] for the diverse members of the church become one body by sharing in Christ's Body and Blood.

Temple of the Spirit

The last metaphor finds its origin in Ephesians: the author describes the church as the household of God, a temple sacred in the Lord, a dwelling place of God in the Spirit (Eph 2:19-22). But the idea of the community as empowered by the Spirit is widespread. For Paul, to be "in Christ," a phrase that appears 164 times in his letters, is to have new life "in the Spirit," enabling Christians to know God's love poured out (cf. Rom 5:5), to call on God as Abba, "Father" (Rom 8:15), and to look forward to a share in his resurrection (Rom 8:11). The church is a community in the Spirit, which enables Christians to confess Jesus as Lord (1 Cor 12:3) and equips the community with a variety of gifts and ministries for its upbuilding (1 Cor 12:4-7).

Thus to be "in Christ," should not be understood in an exclusively individual sense, as it often is today. Being in Christ "does not mean a purely individual relationship between Christ and the believer. It means belonging to the realm within which Christ rules, and that realm is his body, the community."[4] Thus the reference of the phrase is primarily ecclesiological. Luke's Acts of the Apostles shows how the Spirit guides the church in its expansion "to the ends of the earth" (Acts 1:8). The Johannine literature presents the church as a community of disciples guided by the Spirit, though it places less emphasis on the emerging institutional aspects of the church, evident in other later New Testament books.

The Catholic Church

As the apostles and witnesses to the life and resurrection of Jesus passed from the scene, the more fluid situation of the earliest communities gave way to a process of institutionalization. The communities began to develop their organizational structures and to take steps to safeguard the faith "handed down" (*paradotheisē*)—what would later be called the apostolic tradition. Protestant scholars have referred to this period, evident in New Testament books such as Colossians and Ephesians, 1 and 2 Timothy, Titus, Acts, Jude, 2 Peter, and the Johannine letters, as "early Catholicism." For example, in the context of a discussion on the role of bishops and deacons, 1 Timothy 3:15 speaks of the church as "the pillar and bulwark of the truth." For many Protestant scholars, "early Catholicism" is a pejorative term because it reflects Catholic concerns for church structure—the transmission of office, the teaching responsibility of pastors, especially the presbyter-bishops, and the importance of preserving the apostolic tradition.[5] Yet it was precisely these emerging structures that played a major role in safeguarding, canonizing, and handing on the Christian literature that became the New Testament. The threefold ministry of a bishop, assisted by presbyters and deacons, was in place at Antioch and some other churches by the end of the first century. By the end of the second century it had spread throughout the church.

As early as 110, Ignatius of Antioch described the church as "catholic," using an adjective derived from the Greek *kat' holos*, "according to the whole": "Wheresoever the bishop shall appear, there let the people be; even as where Jesus may be, there is the universal [*katholikē*] Church" (Smyrn 8:2). By the mid–second century, the adjective "catholic" is being used to distinguish the true church from various heretical and schismatic groups, a usage found also in Augustine (354–430).[6] Bringing several senses of the word together, Cyril of Jerusalem (d. 387) described the church as catholic because it extends to the ends of the earth, teaches all the doctrines necessary for salvation, instructs all peoples, heals every kind of sin, and possesses every virtue (*Catechesis* 18).

The papacy, Catholicism's most obvious symbol, was slower to develop, though it has ancient roots. Peter, who was originally called Simon, stands out in the New Testament. He was first among the disciples, and several traditions show Jesus giving Peter a special role or commission; he gives Peter the keys as the rock (*petra*) on which he will build his church (Matt 16:18-19; cf. Luke 22:31-32; John 21:15-17), prays for him that he might strengthen his brothers (Luke 22:31-34), and commissions him to be the pastor of the flock (John 21:15-17).

After the fall of Jerusalem in 70 CE, Rome becomes the first church, distinguished by its unique apostolic heritage, claiming both Peter and Paul for their work and martyrdom there. Even within the New Testament period Rome was instructing other churches, evident from the First Letter of Peter, written from Rome in Peter's name to churches in Asia Minor in the 80s, and First Clement, written by a leader of the Roman church to the church of Corinth in the year 96. Shortly after this Ignatius of Antioch wrote in his letter to the church of Rome, "You have taught others" (Rom 3:1). Rome was seen as *the* apostolic see and a privileged norm for the apostolic tradition. According to Irenaeus of Lyon (ca. 180), "it is a matter of necessity that every church should agree with this church, on account of its pre-eminent authority" (*Adversus haereses* 3.3.2). By the later fourth century the bishops of Rome were claiming succession to Peter; by the fifth they had reserved the title "pope" for themselves, and from then on a council had to be in union with the bishop of Rome to be considered valid.

From the beginning the concept of communion or fellowship (*koinōnia*) played a key role in the understanding of church. The Greek word *koinōnia* means to share or participate in something else; it is translated by participation, communion, or fellowship. For Paul *koinōnia* indicated the bond of a shared life; Christians have communion with Christ as a gift of God (1 Cor 1:9), through sharing in the gospel (Phil 1:5), in faith (Phlm 6), and in the Spirit (2 Cor 13:13). There is an essentially ecclesial dimension to *koinōnia*; because we have a share or participation in the Body and Blood of Jesus we are united as his body (1 Cor 10:16-17). Luke uses *koinōnia* to describe the "communal life" of the primitive community in Jerusalem (Acts 2:42).

The early church witnessed to its unity through visible signs of communion: eucharistic hospitality, letters of communion for travelers, communion between the bishops, the practice of the *fermentum* (sending a particle of bread from the bishop or pope's Eucharist to the bishops of neighboring churches), and as early as the third century communion with Rome. The requirement that at least three bishops participate in the ordination of a new bishop symbolized that his church was in communion with the other bishops and their churches. Thus the ancient church was a communion of churches. Conversely, those who damaged the communion of the church through schism or serious sin were "excommunicated."

Three Great Turning Points

As the church continued to grow and change, its history has been marked by three great turning points, the Gregorian Reform in the eleventh century, the Reformation in the sixteenth, and the Second Vatican Council in the twentieth.

The Gregorian Reform

The Gregorian Reform takes its name from Pope Gregory VII (1073–85), who was its major figure. It represented an attempt to win back and safeguard the freedom of the church from domination by feudal lords and secular authorities. Thus it targeted the sale of clerical offices and estates (simony), the appointment of bishops by secular rulers (lay investiture), as well as clerical concubinage. While it sought to support the authority of local bishops and metropolitans in making episcopal appointments, political pressures increasingly resulted in appeals to Rome. In an effort to depoliticize the papacy, the reform also restructured the College of Cardinals into an international administrative council that would henceforth elect the pope. Though not its original intention, the reform had the effect of an increasingly centralized church, inaugurating the modern papacy.

The Reformation

The Reformation in the sixteenth century is a complex story of various movements in the Western church, driven by different theological, political, and national forces. It began in Germany with Luther's rediscovery of the doctrine of justification by faith and was carried out with the support of the German princes, though Luther himself never intended to establish another church. The Reformed movement in France and Switzerland was spearheaded by Ulrich Zwingli and John Calvin and found its theological focus in Calvin's *Institutes of the Christian Religion.* The Church of England, created by an act of Parliament making the British sovereign in the person of Henry VIII head of the Church of England, emerged out of Henry's dispute with the pope over his marriage to Catherine of Aragon.

The so-called Radical Reformation, best symbolized by the Anabaptists, traces its roots to the Swiss Brethren and the leadership of Menno Simons. Opposing both the Catholic Church and the Reformers, the Anabaptists rejected infant baptism in favor of "believer's baptism" and sought to live communally in the manner of the apostolic church of the New Testament. Descendants of the Anabaptists include the Mennonites; the Baptists, originating in England under John Smyth; and the Free Church tradition. Common to all these movements was granting an absolute authority to Scripture, against the authority of the church. The tragedy of the Reformation is that by the time the Catholic Church responded to the clear need for reform by summoning the Council of Trent (1545–47; 1551–52; 1561–63), half of Europe had become Protestant. In the following centuries, the church became more and more defensive in the face of what it saw as an increasingly secular world and the hostile culture of modernity.

The Second Vatican Council

When the seventy-six-year-old Angelo Roncalli was elected as John XXIII in 1958, he was supposed to be a transitional pope. But this compromise candidate surprised everyone by summoning the more than 2,500 bishops of the church together for the Second Vatican Council (1962–65). He set two goals for the council: first, he wanted to call all the churches to seek again the unity for which so many yearned; and second, in specifying that the council was to be pastoral rather than doctrinal, he initiated the internal renewal or *aggiornamento* of the Catholic Church.

In many ways the council symbolized the Catholic Church finally coming to terms with modernity. Departing from the neoscholasticism so long characteristic of Roman theology, its documents reflected an acceptance of modern historical-critical ways of thinking. The Declaration on Religious Freedom (*Dignitatis Humanae*) affirmed modernity's principle of religious liberty, rooted in the dignity of the human person (DH 2). The Decree on Ecumenism (*Unitatis Redintegratio*) for the first time asked pardon of other Christians for Catholic sins against unity (UR 7) and committed the Catholic Church to the ecumenical movement. Its Declaration on the Relationship of the Church to Non-Christian Religions (*Nostra Aetate*) adopted a new, positive attitude toward interreligious dialogue. Without renouncing its responsibility for proclaiming Christ as "the way, and the truth, and the life" (John 14:6), the document approaches the precepts and teachings of the non-Christian religions with reverence, acknowledging that they often reflect a ray of divine truth (NA 2). Finally, the Pastoral Constitution on the Church in the Modern

World (*Gaudium et Spes*) abandoned the defensive posture that so often characterized the church in its battle with modernity, turning it toward the world and especially toward the poor. In the years following the council the emphasis on social justice and the theologies of liberation would find their inspiration in this document.

The sixteen documents produced by the council were to transform Catholic life within a generation.[7] The Dogmatic Constitution on the Church (*Lumen Gentium*) moves from the juridical, "perfect society" model of Vatican I to present the church in biblical, sacramental, and collegial terms. It introduces the church as "in the nature of sacrament—a sign and instrument, that is, of communion with God and of unity among all" (LG 1). Several themes stand out.

Chapter 2 treats the whole church as the people of God, enriched with diverse "gifts" or "charisms" (LG 12). In regard to people who do not share the faith of Christians, the constitution affirmed that those "who, through no fault of their own, do not know the Gospel of Christ or his Church, but who nevertheless seek God with a sincere heart, and, moved by grace, try in their actions to do his will as they know it through the dictates of their conscience—those too may achieve eternal salvation" (LG 16).

Chapter 3 develops a collegial theology of the episcopal office. Like the apostles, the bishops constitute a body or college that with the pope exercises supreme authority over the universal church (LG 22), while each bishop, as an ordinary, is placed in charge of a particular church (LG 23). Reinterpreting Vatican I on papal infallibility, it taught that the bishops when united with the pope share in the church's infallible teaching office (LG 25). They are not to be considered vicars of the pope but govern the churches assigned to them (LG 27).

Chapter 4 develops a theology of the laity in the church; laypersons do not merely cooperate in the apostolate that is proper to the hierarchy but share in the church's mission through baptism and confirmation (LG 33), and thus in the threefold mission of Christ as prophet, priest, and king (LG 31). This laid the foundation for the explosion of lay ministries in the postconciliar church. Chapter five emphasizes that not just priests and religious, but all Christians are called to holiness.

The Dogmatic Constitution on Divine Revelation (*Dei Verbum*) taught that God's self-communication in history, witnessed to in Scripture, reaches its fullness in the person of Jesus (DV 2). Thus its view of revelation is personal rather than propositional; revelation is trinitarian in form, christological in its fulfillment, and historical in its mediation. Correct interpretation of Scripture involves a concern for the biblical author's intention, implying the importance of historical-critical study, though under the guidance of the church (DV 12).

The Constitution on the Sacred Liturgy (*Sacrosanctum Concilium*) has had perhaps the most dramatic impact on Catholic life. It encouraged the renewal of the church's official prayer and worship, providing for full participation by the people (SC 30), simplifying the rites (SC 34), stressing the sermon or homily as part of the liturgy (SC 35), and opening the way to vernacular translations (SC 36).

The Church as Communion

The council also took important steps toward recovering the theology of communion that characterized the way the church understood itself in the first millennium. Though the theme of the church as a communion is not explicitly developed in the council's documents, it is the perspective that underlies its fundamental ecclesiological vision, and it would be further articulated in the years after the council. The council spoke of the bishops as heads of local or "particular" churches. As vicars and legates of Christ they govern "the particular churches assigned to them" (LG 27), while together "with their head, the Supreme Pontiff, and never apart from him, they have supreme and full authority over the universal church" (LG 22), exercising with him the "infallibility promised to the church" (LG 25).

Yet the council was careful to add that the assent of the church can never be wanting to the resulting definitions of pope and bishops "on account of the same Holy Spirit's influence, through which Christ's whole flock is maintained in the unity of the faith and makes progress in it" (LG 25). Implicit here is the doctrine of the *sensus fidelium*, the sense of the faithful by which the Spirit continues to guide the church and keep it in the truth. The church is thus not divided into a two-level, top-down teaching church (*ecclesia docens*) and a learning church (*ecclesia discens*), as an older ecclesiology would have it, but is envisioned as an organic communion in which the Spirit guides both faithful and bishops into the fullness of the faith.

Thus the council's teaching on the church made possible a retrieval of the theology of communion (*koinōnia*) so important to the church of the first millennium. The 1985 Extraordinary Synod of Bishops states that the Catholic Church has fully assumed its ecumenical responsibility on the basis of the ecclesiology of communion.[8] The church is a communion of churches, maintained in unity by the communion between the bishops themselves and with the bishop of Rome who presides over the churches in love. This has involved a shift in the ecclesiological self-understanding of many Catholics. To be a Catholic is not to be a member of a monolithic, global church, but to be a member of a local church in the communion of the *ecclesia catholica*, the church catholic.

Communion also describes the relationship of the individual to the church. To be in full communion is to share fully in the church's life, expressed in the ancient church by the signs of communion we considered earlier, and to participate in its Eucharist. The council taught that non-Catholic Christians are brought into partial communion with the Catholic Church through baptism (UR 3) and are linked to the Catholic Church by faith and the Holy Spirit (LG 15). "Fully incorporated" into the church means accepting "all the means of salvation" established in the Catholic Church, including its faith, sacraments, ecclesiastical government, and communion (LG 14); therefore it is more correct to speak of "converts" being received into full communion with the Catholic Church, while the goal of the ecumenical movement is to reestablish full communion among all the churches and ecclesial communities.

These bonds of communion, uniting faithful, bishops, and pope have preserved the Catholic Church as a communion of churches—or in more secular terms—as an international institution now nearly two thousand years old. The genius of Catholicism has been precisely its historic ability to maintain unity in diversity—the particular and the universal, primacy and conciliarity, the local churches and the communion of the church.

Conclusion

The church is never just isolated individuals, or even a single congregation; it can be described as a global community of memory, passing on, interpreting, and coming to a deeper understanding of the mystery of Jesus from which it lives. To see the church as a communion is to recognize that we have a shared life with God in Christ and therefore with one another. These relations that join us are primarily spiritual, though they often take on institutional expression. They preserve the Catholic Church with its more than a billion members as a communion of diverse churches, united by bonds of love and communion, at the service of the kingdom of God. It is the world's oldest institution.

The challenge for the future is how to maintain and indeed expand that communion into a true communion of communions. Karl Rahner once observed that the Second Vatican Council represented the transformation of Western Christianity, a church largely of Europe and North America, into a world church.[9] As the churches of Africa, Asia, and Latin America, no longer dependent on Western missionaries, begin to develop their own indigenous, "contextual" theologies, the challenge for Rome is to find ways to balance the local with the universal, regional churches with Roman authority. As these regional churches begin to address problems unique to their local situations, finding in effect their own voice, conflicts will be inevitable.

As early as 1984 the Vatican's Congregation for the Doctrine of the Faith (CDF) published an instruction, On Certain Aspects of the Theology of Liberation, raising questions about what it saw as a too facile Latin American embrace of certain Marxist concepts, identifying the kingdom of God with the movement for liberation, and challenging the hierarchical nature of the church. A second instruction two years later, Instruction on Christian Freedom and Liberation, was only slightly less critical.

In the United States questions over the role of women in the church and the explosion of lay ministries have raised concerns in Rome. The American bishops tried to write a pastoral letter on women, but after several critical Roman interventions they abandoned the project in 1992.[10] Vatican fears about a diminished sense of the importance of priesthood have resulted in several Roman documents emphasizing the differences between the roles of the laity and the ordained. Similarly, churches in Africa, where the Catholic population has tripled between 1978 and 2004, struggle against clericalism as well as discrimination against women.

Tensions have also arisen between the Vatican and the Federation of Asian Bishops' Conferences (FABC). The bishops of Indonesia have several times asked Rome for permission to ordain married men. Representatives of the FABC criticized the documents prepared by Rome for the 1998 Synod of Bishops for Asia for being too "Western" in their approach. Among other things, Rome insisted that the Asian churches proclaim salvation though Christ alone, an approach the Asian bishops found a poor starting point for their Asian context. Tensions over this and other issues led to the CDF's 2000 declaration, *Dominus Iesus*, which insisted on the uniqueness of Christ and argued that members of other religions are "objectively speaking . . . in a gravely deficient situation in comparison to those in the church" (no. 22). Subsequently the CDF has published several "notifications" raising questions about the positions of Jacques Dupuis (2001), Roger Haight (2004), and Jon Sobrino (2006) on religious pluralism, and it has recently begun an investigation of Peter Phan (2007).

Such tensions between the Roman center and distant churches in very different cultures will no doubt reoccur in the years ahead, let alone in the more distant future when hopefully other communions will enter into communion with Rome. But they are also a sign of the vitality of the church, whose center of gravity is now shifting to the southern hemisphere. Living as a more inclusive world communion will also challenge Rome to reform the way it exercises authority, conducts synods, and intervenes in regional churches.

At the same time, as a world church with a developed social teaching, international structures, synods, religious orders, and lay movements, and a universal spokesman for the church in the person of the pope, the Catholic Church is uniquely positioned to witness to the kingdom of God in an era characterized by globalization. The challenge is to find ways to maintain the bonds between the local and the universal in a communion that is truly catholic, not merely in its geographical extension, but in its fullness, embracing all legitimate expressions of life in Christ.

For Reflection

• What is the relationship between the ministry of Jesus and the church?
• How do you understand the biblical metaphors for church (People of God, Body of Christ, and Temple of the Spirit)?
• What does it mean to live in communion with the church?
• In what sense can the church become more catholic?

Scripture Passages

Exodus 19:1-6	Matthew 18	Mark 10:35-45
Luke 6:20-36	Romans 6:3-23	1 Corinthians 10:16-17
1 Corinthians 11:23-26	Ephesians 1:15–2:22	1 Peter 2:4-10

Recommended Readings

Clark, Edward Wm. *Five Great Catholic Ideas*. New York: Crossroad, 1998.

Doyle, Dennis M. *Communion Ecclesiology: Vision and Versions*. Maryknoll, NY: Orbis Books, 2000.

Dulles, Avery. *Models of the Church*. Garden City, NY: Doubleday, 1974.

Gaillardetz, Richard R. *By What Authority? A Primer on Scripture, the Magisterium, and the Sense of the Faithful*. Collegeville, MN: Liturgical Press, 2003.

Markey, John J. *Creating Communion: The Theology of the Constitution on the Church*. Hyde Park, NY: New City Press, 2003.

Rausch, Thomas P. *Towards a Truly Catholic Church*. Collegeville, MN: Liturgical Press, 2005.

Ruddy, Christopher. *The Local Church: Tillard and the Future of Catholic Ecclesiology*. New York: Crossroad, 2006.

6

Sheila McLaughlin

Lay Ecclesial Ministry

The emergence of lay ecclesial ministry in recent years is an important and exciting development in the life of the church in the United States. Significant numbers of laity are responding to the prompting of the Holy Spirit and the needs of the church in many and varied ways. They have embraced discipleship with Jesus, joining the church in continuing his saving mission of bringing forth the reign of God. Parishes and dioceses in all areas of the country are able to fulfill their mission because dedicated and competent laypeople put their gifts and talents at the service of their communities. In this chapter we will explore the development of lay ecclesial ministry and offer brief reflections on the experience of lay ecclesial ministry in the church today.

Historical Development

Many people believe that lay ministry is a new phenomenon, but in reality it has been part of our tradition since the days of the first Christian communities. We read in the New Testament about the ministry provided by Prisca and Aquila (Acts 18:18, 26) and of Andronicus and Junia, described as "prominent among the apostles" (Rom 16:7). These early disciples were collaborators with Paul and other leaders of the Christian community. As time went on and the church became more structured, leadership roles were reserved for the ordained. The mission of the laity was to be Christ in the world, bringing his presence to the marketplace, the school, the office. Laypeople tended to be excluded from ministerial functions and viewed as having a subordinate role in the church. Despite this, various movements of laity within the church, such as Catholic Action, developed and grew during the twentieth century. The groundbreaking work of theologians like Yves Congar contributed to a renewed understanding of the mission of the laity and the relationship between the laity and the ordained within the church.[1]

The Second Vatican Council made a very significant contribution to the renewal of the theology of the laity. The vision of the council concerning the laity is found especially in the Dogmatic Constitution on the Church (*Lumen Gentium*) and the Decree on the Apostolate of the Laity (*Apostolicam Actuositatem*).[2] In the debates at the council, many bishops emphasized the need to articulate a more positive and biblically based understanding of the role of the laity in the church. The council taught that through baptism all Christians share in the priestly, prophetic, and royal offices of Christ and therefore in the mission of the church in the world (LG 33–36). Employing the term "apostolate" rather than "ministry," the bishops said that the call to apostolic work comes directly from Christ and flows from the sacraments of initiation: "The apostolate of the laity is a sharing in the salvific mission of the Church. Through Baptism and Confirmation all are appointed to this apostolate by the Lord himself" (LG 33). The council recognized and affirmed the indispensable and distinct role of the laity in promoting justice and peace in the world as well as building up the Body of Christ in the church.

The bishops at Vatican II made the important decision to write a separate document on the laity. Building on what they had written in *Lumen Gentium*, they say, "From the fact of their union with Christ the head flows the lay[person's] right and duty to be apostles" (AA 3). Once again, they ground this vocation in the sacraments of initiation. The bishops make reference to the biblical doctrine of the "priesthood of the faithful" (1 Pet 2:4-10)—a teaching that had been downplayed in official Catholic theology since the time of the Protestant Reformation. While the laity play a unique role in spreading the reign of God in the world, the council did not confine their apostolate to the "secular" realm. The bishops state, "The laity, carrying out this mission of the Church, exercise their apostolate therefore in the world as well as in the Church, in the temporal order as well as the spiritual" (AA 5). This decree extends the work of the laity to "the apostolate of evangelization and sanctification" (AA 31). These teachings of Vatican II provided a solid foundation for the further developments in the theology of lay ministry that have taken place since the council.

In 1987 a synod of bishops met to discuss the topic of the laity in the church. Preparatory consultations were held all over the world, including meetings in the United States that drew 250,000 Catholics.[3] From the discussions at this synod, Pope John Paul II wrote an apostolic exhortation titled The Lay Members of Christ's Faithful People (Christifideles Laici). The pope likened laypeople in the church to the laborers in the vineyard in the story told by Jesus (Matt 20:1-16). He observed, "The gospel parable sets before our eyes the Lord's vast vineyard and the multitude of persons, both women and men, who are called and sent forth by him to labor in it. The vineyard is the whole world (Matt 13:38) which is to be transformed according to the plan of God in view of the final coming of the Kingdom of God" (CL 1). The pope proceeds to teach that laypeople are called by Christ "to take an active, conscientious and responsible part in the mission of the Church in this great moment of history" (CL 3). He emphasizes that "[it] is not permissible for anyone to remain idle" (CL 3). This parable of the vineyard workers recalls the rich biblical image of the vine. In the Gospel of John, Jesus describes himself as the vine and his disciples as the branches (John 15:1-17). Living in Christ—remaining vitally connected to him—empowers believers to fulfill their vocation to participate in the mission of the church.

In this same document, Pope John Paul appeals to the teaching of Vatican II about the universal call to holiness (LG 39–42). Fidelity to this fundamental vocation on the part of all Christians is essential for the renewal of the church and the world. This call to holiness is rooted in baptism and confirmation and nourished through the Eucharist, the source and summit of Christian life. The Eucharist, our Holy Communion, brings about communion among all the members of the Body of Christ. About this communion in the church the pope says, "Ecclesial communion is more precisely likened to an 'organic' communion, analogous to that of a living and functioning body. In fact, at one and the same time it is characterized by a *diversity* and a *complementarity* of vocations and states in life, of ministries, of charisms and responsibilities. Because of this diversity and complementarity every member of the lay faithful is seen *in relation to the whole body* and *offers a totally unique contribution* on behalf of the whole body" (CL 20). Each of us, in whatever way we minister, does so in relationship to the entire Body of Christ and all its ministers, and each of us has his or her own contribution to make.

Every ministry in the church is inspired and empowered by the grace of God in Christ. The call to serve the people of God is a gift that comes from God. Pope John Paul adduces the Letter to the Ephesians in underlining the grace of ministry and the diversity of ministerial gifts in the church: "But each of us was given grace according to the measure of Christ's gift. . . . The gifts he gave were that some would be apostles, some prophets, some evangelists, some pastors and teachers, to equip the saints for the work of ministry, for building up the body of Christ, until all of us come to the unity of faith and of the knowledge of the Son of God, to maturity, to the measure of the full stature of Christ" (Eph 4:7, 11-13).

Christifideles Laici also describes a variety of ways that the lay faithful can exercise pastoral ministry, such as the ministry of the word, presiding over liturgical prayers, conferring baptism, and distributing Holy Communion. It recognizes the contribution of the laity in the work of evangelization and in the renewal of the liturgy (CL 20). The document speaks of the charisms of the

Holy Spirit as "graces of the Holy Spirit that have, directly or indirectly, a usefulness for the ecclesial community, ordered as they are to the building up of the church, to the well-being of humanity and to the needs of the world" (CL 24). The charisms are to be accepted in gratitude by the one who receives them, and by the entire church. Laypersons are encouraged to undertake ministry according to their particular gifts and charisms. All, regardless of age or gender, have an important contribution to make to the church's mission.

Lay Ecclesial Ministry in the United States

Over the past thirty years, the bishops of the United States have been engaged in serious reflection regarding the role of lay ecclesial ministry within the church. In 1980, the United States Conference of Catholic Bishops issued a statement titled Called and Gifted,[4] which acknowledged the many ways laymen and laywomen answer the Lord's call and use their gifts in the service of the church. In particular, this document addressed the laity's call to holiness, adulthood, ministry, and community and began to use the term *lay ecclesial ministry* to describe the leadership or professional ministry provided by those with specialized training. In 1995, an updated statement was published by the USCCB titled Called and Gifted for the Third Millennium. Here the bishops described the large and growing numbers of laypeople involved in various ministries, especially in the liturgy. They noted the significant numbers of the faithful serving in the liturgy as lectors, ministers of communion, members of liturgy planning teams, sacristans, and servers. They also recognized those who teach and mentor young people and adults, serve in peace and justice networks, and provide sacramental preparation and bereavement ministry.

The USCCB document points out that in 1995 most parishes reported having laypeople or vowed religious in pastoral staff positions, and some parishes had been entrusted to a layperson in the absence of a resident pastor. A ritual book for a Sunday

Celebration in the Absence of a Priest was in common use at this time. According to those surveyed, the pastoral needs of God's people were being ably and generously served by many kinds of lay ecclesial ministers. The ministers themselves spoke of their work as a calling, not merely a job. They expressed the belief that God had called them to their ministries and reported that it was often their parish priest who helped them discern their call.[5]

In 1998, in an effort to seek further clarity about both *what* lay ecclesial ministers were doing, and *why* they were doing it, the USCCB published a collection of papers from a colloquium on lay ecclesial ministry titled Together in God's Service: Towards a Theology of Ecclesial Lay Ministry. The first of these papers is an overview of lay ecclesial ministry by Zeni Fox, a theologian and well-known expert on lay ministry.[6] According to Fox, at that time 60 percent of the lay ecclesial ministers serving in positions around the country described their work as ministry; they did not use job or career language to describe what they were doing. In parishes, it was common to find them serving as pastoral associates and as directors of religious education, liturgy, music, social concerns, and youth ministry. On the diocesan level, they held the positions of chancellor, superintendent of schools, and directors of religious education, worship, and lay formation. The majority reported being happy in their work, and they found their ministry satisfying and spiritually rewarding. These ministers understood themselves to be called by God to engage in their particular ministries, to use their God-given gifts to respond to the needs of God's people. Most of them believed that the authority to perform their ministry came from their baptism and confirmation, from their training and competence, and from a call given by God.

The ongoing conversation about laity in ministry, as well as the fruits of the rich experience of lay ecclesial ministers, contributed significantly to the development of the 2005 statement of the U.S. Catholic bishops, Co-Workers in the Vineyard of the Lord: A Resource for Guiding the Development of Lay Ecclesial Ministry.[7] This document represents a significant development of the conversation around lay ecclesial ministry. It offers further definition and clarity, though it does not promote norms or establish church law. It is a resource that provides pastoral and theological reflection on lay ecclesial ministry, an affirmation of those who serve in this capacity, and a synthesis of best thinking and practice. It is intended to provide a framework that will ensure that the continuing development of lay ecclesial ministry will be faithful to the church's teaching and respond to the needs of the church. The document reiterates the teaching of Vatican II about the call to holiness and the transformation of the world. It begins with the vision and challenge expressed by Pope John Paul II in a letter he wrote for the Jubilee Year 2000:

> The unity of the Church is not uniformity, but an organic blending of legitimate diversities. It is the reality of many members joined in a single body, the one Body of Christ (1 Cor 12:12). Therefore the Church of the Third Millennium will need to encourage all the baptized and confirmed to be aware of their active responsibility in the Church's life. Together with the ordained ministry, other ministries, whether formally instituted or simply recognized, can flourish for the good of the whole community, sustaining it in all its many needs: from catechesis to liturgy, from education of the young to the widest array of charitable works.[8]

Co-Workers in the Vineyard of the Lord represents the most recent official statement on lay ecclesial ministry in the United States. Therefore it is important to enumerate its key points. Co-Workers recognizes lay ecclesial ministry as a true calling of the Holy Spirit, rooted in baptism to serve the church and its mission. Lay ecclesial ministers are those whose service is characterized by:

1. Authorization of the hierarchy to serve publicly in the local church

2. Leadership in a particular area of ministry

3. Close mutual collaboration with the pastoral ministry of bishops, priests, and deacons

4. Preparation and formation appropriate to the level of responsibilities that are assigned to them

The term "lay ecclesial minister" is meant to be generic. It is not a specific title nor does it imply a new rank among the laity. As mentioned above, it encompasses numerous roles, such as director of music or liturgy, pastoral associate, school principal, and so forth. These are roles of leadership. This term does not apply to a variety of other ministries in the community, such as serving at a soup kitchen or shelter, or the many ways laypeople live out their baptismal call in the world. It is up to the local bishop to determine which roles in the diocese will be considered for this designation, and, based on particular needs, they may vary from diocese to diocese.

Co-Workers offers a succinct definition of lay ecclesial ministry. This ministry is "lay" because it is carried out by laypersons and has as its sacramental basis the sacraments of initiation. It is ecclesial because it is situated within the community of the church, whose communion and mission it serves, and because it is subject to the authority of the church's hierarchy. It is ministry because it entails a participation in the threefold ministry of Christ, who is priest, prophet, and king. It is not intended to be a sharing in the ministry of the ordained, but rather a distinct service performed in communion with ordained ministers. Lay ministry is distinctly different from ordained ministry, yet each is a participation in the priesthood of Christ. Professional competence is required, therefore academic preparation, certification, credentialing, and formation are necessary.

Lay ministry, like all ministry, finds its place within the communion of the church and serves the mission of Christ. "Communion and mission provide the foundation for understanding and carrying out lay ecclesial ministry."[9] The communion of the Trinity is the source of the church's mission to bring about the reign of God. An ecclesiology of communion looks upon different gifts and functions not as adversarial but as enriching and complementary. It appreciates the church's unity as an expression of the mutual and reciprocal gifts brought into harmony by the Holy Spirit (CL 20). Because lay ecclesial ministry is situated within the communion of the church and has a public character, it requires the authorization of the bishop.

In Co-Workers the bishops also address the question of how one determines the authenticity of a call to lay ecclesial ministry. A process of discernment is necessary. Often this begins with a personal invitation from a pastor or other parish minister, or perhaps a friend, who recognizes in that person a capacity to serve God's people. The discernment process is both personal and communal and involves retreats and days of prayer, as well as individual and group spiritual direction. A helpful resource in the discernment process is the USCCB publication, National Certification Standards for Lay Ecclesial Ministers Serving as Parish Catechetical Directors, Youth Ministry Leaders, Pastoral Associates, and Parish Life Coordinators.

Co-Workers emphasizes that formation is essential for lay ministry. It highlights four dimensions of formation for ministry: human, spiritual, intellectual, and pastoral. It says that human formation "seeks to develop the lay ecclesial minister's human qualities and character, fostering a healthy and well-balanced personality for the sake of both personal growth and ministerial service."[10] All involved in ministry need sound character, psychological and physical health, a mature understanding of sexuality, and insight into their particular gifts.

Spiritual formation is essential because ministry must be based on a personal encounter and ongoing relationship with the Lord, nurtured by God's word, the sacraments, and a life dedicated to prayer. Given the varied responsibilities of many lay ministers, especially those with families, finding time to set aside for prayer can be challenging. Our rich Catholic tradition offers a wide variety of spiritual practices. Each of us needs to find the spirituality that suits us. A spiritual director can be of great help for growth in our life with God. Success and fulfillment come through prayer and participation in the sacraments, especially the Eucharist.

The intellectual formation for lay ecclesial ministers is to be "as broad and deep as possible, with exposure to the vast range of topics and subjects that constitute Catholic theology."[11] Programs should include Scripture, dogmatic theology, church history, liturgical and sacramental theology, moral theology and Catholic social teaching, pastoral theology, spirituality, and canon law. In response to this need, growing numbers of theological programs have been established around the country for men and women preparing for lay ecclesial ministry.

The pastoral skills necessary for leadership in ministry are varied and quite extensive. They include: leadership of prayer and preaching; effective relationship and communication skills; the ability to collaborate effectively with others in ministry; an understanding of current social, political, and cultural realities in light of the gospel; discernment of gifts, our own and those of others in our communities; conflict resolution skills; administrative skills; leadership and organizational development. In addition, there is the need for ongoing formation for even the most experienced ministers in order to continually nurture one's spiritual life, maintain awareness of important developments in the life and teaching of the church, and keep skills up-to-date.

Ministry is never a "me and God" thing. It always exists within and flows from a community. Thus, authorization of ministers is important, both at the diocesan and parish levels. Rituals and ceremonies affirm, recognize, and celebrate the accomplishments of lay ecclesial ministers in completing their formation programs, and they also give powerful witness to the community of the importance of lay ecclesial ministry.

These documents and statements may seem abstract, or perhaps daunting. Nevertheless, familiarity with them is essential for anyone wanting to understand the theological basis for lay ecclesial ministry and its pastoral requirements. As someone who has been involved in ministry for over twenty-five years, I have seen the way in which the vision has been clarified and expanded as a result of the growth and maturity of lay ecclesial ministry. The last section of Co-Workers can be especially challenging, setting what might seem to be impossible goals that call for every imaginable gift and talent. In reality this articulation of the formational needs for lay ecclesial ministry speaks of the critical importance that the bishops place on this ministry in the life of the church. The leadership of lay ecclesial ministers is crucial to fulfilling the needs of the church in service to God's people, and it demands our best efforts. That is why expectations placed on lay ecclesial ministers are similar to those required for the ordained ministry. No one person will possess all of these in full measure, but all ministers need basic skills in these areas.

Personal Reflections

In conclusion, I would like to offer a few personal reflections on my own experience as a lay ecclesial minister. My ministry as a parish liturgy coordinator began in the early 1980s in response to an invitation extended by my pastor. I had been involved as a volunteer for several years in liturgical ministry and had attended numerous liturgy workshops, but I had no plans to "work" for the church. The pastor needed assistance, and I agreed to help. I certainly did not realize at the time what this decision would mean for my life! Almost immediately I discovered that the position required further education and particular skills, and I enrolled in a two-year certificate program sponsored by the Archdiocesan Office for Divine Worship in Chicago. I quickly became immersed in what was for me the fascinating world of ministry. I didn't know about guidelines for discernment, but rather acted from instinct. I was very aware that something important was going on in my life and I tried to be attentive to the working of the Spirit. It did not take long for me to realize that it was when I was engaged in ministry that I experienced a fullness of joy and peace.

This pattern of invitation/response was very common in those days; most of the women and men with whom I was studying spoke of similar experiences. It was a time of great generosity, of excitement and possibility, when every day there seemed to be new conferences and programs to attend, many sponsored by the flourishing network of organizations dedicated to particular ministries. It is also fair to say that lay ecclesial ministry was not universally accepted. There was resistance to filling key parish and diocesan roles with laypeople, and there were few paying positions in parishes. The church was raising questions about the overall function of these ministers and about their selection, training, certification, and relationship to the ordained. The ministers themselves also had questions about their function and role, their authority to make decisions, collaboration—especially with the ordained—and just labor practices. There was a sense among many parishioners that this was a stopgap measure, necessitated by the declining numbers of clergy, and as such, this ministry would never have legitimacy.

In 1985, Cardinal Joseph Bernardin, archbishop of Chicago, wrote a pastoral letter to address these questions and the sense of confusion about lay ecclesial ministry, titled In Service of One Another.[12] In this statement, he examined many of the issues that were being raised in Chicago, including a number of those named above. In his sensitive and pastoral style, the cardinal acknowledged the tensions, yet he strongly affirmed the development of lay ecclesial ministries. He promised his support to all engaged in any of the church's ministries, encouraged better coordination, and attempted to offer some clarification and direction. In the conclusion of the letter he invites the reader to join with him in a vision for a church preparing for the third millennium of Christianity. He describes this church in a number of ways: "a community of faith over which the risen Lord truly presides"; "a community in which all members, in virtue of their incorporation into Christ through baptism and confirmation, witness to the Lord's saving deeds before the entire world and work for the emergence of the kingdom he proclaimed"; "a community whose designated ministers—laity, religious, priests, deacons and bishops—understand and accept their uniquely different but complementary and necessary roles, working together for the good of all"; "a community in which Jesus' love and mercy, his justice, his compassion and healing power are tangibly evident each day."[13] More important than his inspiring words were his actions, which demonstrated an extraordinary commitment to lay ecclesial ministry. During his tenure as archbishop,

Cardinal Bernardin appointed numerous lay ecclesial ministers, especially women, to positions of leadership in the diocese. My own service as director of the Office for Divine Worship was the result of this commitment. The positions of chief of staff, archdiocesan director of catechetical ministries, superintendent of schools, and director of personnel services were all held by women appointed by him as well.

A study conducted in 2005 reported that there were over thirty thousand lay ecclesial ministers working at least twenty hours per week in paid positions in U.S. parishes. An additional two thousand were ministering in hospitals, other health care settings, colleges and universities, prisons, seaports, and airports. This number represented a 40 percent increase since 1990. Organizations dedicated to particular ministries, such as the National Association of Pastoral Musicians, boast of thousands of members. Lay ecclesial ministers have been embraced by the Catholic community, not because of studies and documents, but because of their faithful and committed service to the people of God. This is clearly not a stopgap measure but rather a full expression of our theology of communion and mission and a cause for rejoicing! To be sure, questions and challenges remain. Serious conversation and discussion will continue. In a recent survey by the National Association for Lay Ministers, workplace issues were reported as a priority.[14] And the critical challenge remains for lay and ordained ministers to understand their roles as complementary so as to foster collaboration and mutual support as they minister together in service of the one mission and ministry of Jesus Christ.

Presently, I serve as the director of the Cardinal Joseph Bernardin Center for Theology and Ministry at Catholic Theological Union. One of my responsibilities is the oversight of the Bernardin Scholars program, which supports lay students preparing for ministry in the church and forms them in the vision and legacy of the late cardinal. Most of the scholars are young people in their twenties and thirties who demonstrate a deep commitment to the Gospel and to serving the church as lay ecclesial ministers. They are incredibly gifted, conscientious, and dedicated to their studies and their ministries. They give us all confidence, hope, and inspiration as we move into the future.

My life of ministry has given me incredible opportunities to work with remarkable women and men of great faith, extraordinary leaders who have inspired and encouraged me and entrusted to me responsibilities that at times I felt were beyond my capabilities. Their mentoring and friendship has been a blessing beyond measure and a key to whatever success I have achieved. I cannot imagine a greater privilege than using one's gifts and talents and spending one's life in service to the mission of Christ.

For Reflection

- What attracts you to a life of ministry?
- What seems most challenging to you about ministry in the church?
- What qualities/gifts/skills can you bring to lay ecclesial ministry?
- What qualities/skills need further development?

Scripture Passages

Matthew 9:35-38	John 15:1-17	Romans 12:1-13
1 Corinthians 12:4-13	Philippians 2:1-4	Ephesians 4:1-7, 11-13
2 Timothy 4:1-5		

Recommended Reading

Fox, Zeni. "Laity, Ministry and Secular Character." In *Ordering the Baptismal Priesthood: Theologies of Lay and Ordained Ministry*, edited by Susan K. Wood, 121–51. Collegeville, MN: Liturgical Press, 2003.

Nilson, Jon. "The Laity." In *The Gift of the Church: A Textbook on Ecclesiology*, edited by Peter Phan, 395–414. Collegeville, MN: Liturgical Press, 2000.

Pope John Paul II. The Lay Members of Christ's Faithful People (*Christifideles Laici*). 1988.

United States Conference of Catholic Bishops. Co-Workers in the Vineyard of the Lord: A Resource for Guiding the Development of Lay Ecclesial Ministry. *Origins* 35, no. 25 (December 1, 2005): 405–27.

Vatican Council II. Decree on the Apostolate of the Laity (*Apostolicam Actuositatem*).

7

Charlene Diorka, SSJ

Religious Life Today

Mary Oliver ends her poem "The Summer Day" asking the poignant question, "Tell me, what is it you plan to do / with your one wild and precious life?"[1] Her ending presents a creative twist to the question each of us asks ourselves as we strive to discover who we are and how God calls us to live in this world. Ultimately, we desire to understand the mystery of God's call; we long to follow our heart, and we want to live with meaning and significance. We hope to live the dream that God is dreaming for us. Knowing that God calls each of us to holiness and does desire our happiness, it is our free choice as to how we will live. Will we marry? Will we remain single? Will we become ordained ministers? Will we follow Jesus as a disciple through the vowed religious life?

What follows is an overview of religious life today. It is by no means comprehensive or exhaustive, but it offers a glimpse into the life commitment in which one chooses to follow Jesus as a vowed priest, brother, or sister in religious life. It describes the unique call of religious life and identifies within this life some particular ways that it can be lived out. It briefly explores the vows of poverty, chastity, and obedience, which are at the heart of this life choice. Likewise, it addresses the essential components of living religious life in the twenty-first century: prayer,

113

ministry, and community living. In addition, it considers how individuals know if they are called to religious life, the process of discernment, and the formative journey that leads to becoming a religious priest, brother, or sister. Finally, it offers some advice for anyone who might be considering religious life.

Sister Sandra Schneiders, IHM, offers a foundational insight into religious life. She explains that one *becomes* a religious. Religious life is not really something that one "enters" or "joins" so much as one lives. It is not something that one does but something that one is.[2] Ultimately, it is a choice of who one will be. It is a choice to leave everything and to follow Jesus. It is a choice about *who* will be the center of one's life in an exclusive and absolute way that determines all other loves and all other choices. In responding to God's invitation to become a consecrated religious, one chooses a uniquely different path to holiness.

Father Pedro Arrupe, SJ, superior general of the Jesuits from 1961 to 1984, poignantly describes this same quality of religious life: "Nothing is more practical than finding God, that is, than falling in love in a quite absolute way. What you are in love with, what seizes your imagination will affect everything. It will decide what will get you out of bed in the mornings, what you will do with your evenings, how you spend your weekends, what you read, who you know, what breaks your heart, and what amazes you with joy and gratitude. Fall in love, stay in love, and it will decide everything."[3]

These words articulate the invitation to follow Jesus in a profound surrender of one's life that yields nothing less than everything. In the Gospel of Mark we read, "Peter began to say to him, 'Look, we have left everything and followed you.' Jesus said, 'Truly I tell you, there is no one who has left house or brothers or sisters or mother or father or children or fields, for my sake and for the sake of the good news, who will not receive a hundredfold now in this age—houses, brothers and sisters, mothers and children, and fields'" (Mark 10:28-30). In choosing to respond to God's call to follow Jesus in religious life, people also choose the style of religious life that best fits their personality and how they desire to be of service.

Types of Religious Communities

Religious life consists of the apostolic, contemplative, cloistered, and monastic ways of living. Apostolic religious communities involve themselves in active ministries. While prayer
and community life are important to them, these religious serve
in a variety of ways—teaching, parish ministry, health care, social work, care for the elderly, work with young people, service
to those who are poor, and many others. The word "apostle"
means to be sent and it implies that these religious are sent
like the apostles to bring the Good News in many diverse and
varied ways. Members of contemplative religious communities
focus on prayer, especially the Mass, praying daily together the
Liturgy of the Hours, and engaging in individual prayer. They
tend to live in greater solitude than members of apostolic communities so that they can better direct their prayer and work
toward contemplation, though some communities that consider
themselves contemplative are also engaged in some active apostolic ministries.[4]

Often, contemplative religious communities are cloistered or
partially cloistered. That is, they live separated from the rest of
the world to be more focused on prayer, including prayer for
the needs of the world. As cloistered religious they rarely leave
their monasteries, and all or most of their work is done within
the monastery itself, depending on the degree to which they
are cloistered. Monastic communities fall somewhere between
apostolic and cloistered. Monastic men and women place a high
value on prayer and community life, but many are also engaged
in active ministries. Monasticism centers on living in community,
common prayer, and Christian meditation.[5]

The Vows

In becoming a religious, no matter what form of religious
life one chooses, a person's commitment takes shape and form
through the countercultural living of the vows of poverty,

chastity, and obedience. When religious profess these vows, they renounce the natural drives for possessions, sex, and power in order to follow in the footsteps of Jesus more closely. These vows are the concrete manifestation of the disciple's "yes" in response to Jesus' invitation to come and follow him. Considered in a positive light, each vow frees the disciple for mission, to be of service to God's people. The vows are less about what is given up or negated and more about what one is freed for. Through the profession of vows, the religious makes a total gift of self to Jesus in response to the great love Jesus offers.

Though each vow is uniquely individual, they are connected and interdependent. Together they enable a free, loving response to Jesus' call. For example, obedience commits religious men and women to listen for God's voice and to be available and ready to respond. The vow of poverty, expressed through a simple lifestyle, helps them to be available and ready to respond to God's voice. Chastity, an exclusive love for God, motivates them to listen for God's voice and respond wholeheartedly in their actions.

The vow of poverty is not about being destitute. Rather, like Jesus, it is about identifying with those who are poor and limiting what one possesses, uses, and needs. This vow calls religious men and women to offer their time, talents, and gifts, in fact, their very person, in union with Jesus for others. It invites the religious to live simply with the basic necessities. This vow helps religious to prioritize what they need over what they want. It transforms the power of ownership and accumulation of possessions into an experience of trust, of being dependent on God and one another for what is necessary. Religious hold all things in common, and they steward and share what is available to them in light of the gospel mandate and the congregational mission. Lived authentically, the vow of poverty leads to healthy detachment from earthly goods, promotes an attitude of gratitude for all that one receives and enables one to enjoy more while having less.

Sister Judith A. Merkle, SNDdeN, in her book, *A Different Touch: A Study of Vows in Religious Life* offers a contemporary and concise way of looking at the vow of poverty. She states, "Today poverty in religious life often means in practice access to enough money to live modestly. One is required to work over the course of one's life, to earn enough so that the community can be independent from other groups and accomplish its mission. This means to live in such a way that each sister or brother can have the modicum of health care, leisure, knowledge, and so on that is needed for the full development of the body and mind and spirit, and the community as a whole can foster a mission outside itself to those in need."[6]

The vow of chastity is often reduced to foregoing marriage, genital sex, and children. While these are real sacrifices that religious make in light of their commitment to Jesus as the absolute in their life, they are not the only defining aspects of the vow of chastity. In fact, the vow is broader and deeper in its context. It calls the religious to a profound and personal relationship with Jesus through prayer, to love all people with the love with which God has loved them, and to be ready, available, and free to go where sent on mission. Chastity points to union with God as the only way that the deep human longing for love can be satisfied. The vow does not nullify the need for friendship, intimacy, and love. Rather it is a life-giving choice to live these aspects of sexuality in a radically different way than our culture proposes. Christopher West, in *Heaven's Song*, highlights the heart of the vow of chastity for celibates when he acknowledges, "Those who consecrate themselves entirely to God as celibates witness to a greater union with their very lives. By doing so, they do not reject their sexuality. Rather, they show us the ultimate purpose and meaning of human sexuality: to point us to union with God."[7]

Chastity calls religious men and women to develop all human qualities and use them for the fostering of life. Religious give and receive love, have male and female friends, and embrace their sexuality in all its fullness. Today, religious are not removed or protected from the culture in which they live. They willingly accept the responsibility to make choices with discretion regarding culture and media. While recognizing the need to be well read and informed, they also critically sift the messages that come through media and influence our culture. Lived faithfully, the vow of chastity disposes one to love many people, generates life in creative and varied ways, and develops a deeply personal and intimate relationship with Jesus that is just as real and sustaining as any human relationship could be. The vow of chastity lived in celibate community points to the world to come and witnesses that God is the only absolute.

The vow of obedience calls for a listening and discerning heart. Through this vow religious men and women promise to listen for God's voice through prayer and discernment as well as through the voice of other members in the community, those entrusted with authority in the congregation, and the events of daily life. It is not so much about blind obedience as it is following where God leads. Sister Kathy Rooney, SSJ, describes how the vow of obedience disposes the religious to be sent. She says, "By virtue of this promise, the congregation asks a member to look beyond personal desires and preferences and to consider the common and greater good."[8] By virtue of the vow of obedience, religious place themselves at the service of the people of God wherever congregational leaders mission them.

Both in making and in accepting decisions, the call in this vow is to seek to know God's will through personal and communal discernment and to trust the decision in a spirit of faith. Members of religious communities look to their congregation's constitutions for the guidelines that help them to live their consecrated life faithfully. Constitutions are the formal documents of each congregation that explain its nature, mission, and purpose along with particular details regarding areas significant to their life such as prayer, governance, membership, vows, and community life. Furthermore, obedience calls religious men and women to participate in all the levels of congregational involvement, bringing initiative, judgment, and personal responsibility. Lived with integrity, the vow of obedience frees one from self-interest, enables one to do the will of God, and leads to fidelity in the work of advancing the kingdom of God.

All in all, the vowed life is one way of life, not better or less than any other way. It is however, a unique way of following in the footsteps of Jesus ever more closely. These vows call each religious man and woman to live counter to the basic human drives to possess, to love in an exclusive way, and to exercise power. They provide a way for those called to religious life to unite themselves with the poor, chaste, and obedient Jesus. At the same time, they call for a continual spirit of reflection and renewal in order that they may remain relevant for each time and place in which they are professed.

Community Life

As you might imagine, the vowed life is not easily lived in isolation; nor is it meant to be. Each member who is striving to live this style of life helps to support and sustain the other. And so the communal dimension of the life is essential to the religious vocation. For example, the Constitutions of the Sisters of Saint Joseph say, "We live in community in a house of our congregation to be a sign of Christian unity and to be a creative and healing presence in our world. We are called to love one another since we are united, not only by the same faith, but also by the same vows and manner of life. We are formed into one body in order that, like the early Christians, we may have but one heart and one mind, one vision in God."[9]

In order to be united in community life in spirit and mission it is important to establish structures and to share in decision making to facilitate living together. Essentially, community living enables religious men and women to seek opportunities to be together, to spend time with one another. Concretely, they share prayer, engage in the routine of daily life, take care of the household tasks, celebrate life's joys, and companion each other in their sorrows. Community does not replace one's family of origin, but it can provide the support and structure to live this celibate, poor, and obedient life. Not unlike the relationship forged through the marital commitment, the commitment lived out through daily communal living is a call to love for better or for worse. Members of community strive to accept, love, and reverence one another in both their strengths and weaknesses. The challenge for community members is to be realistic in their expectations of one another and patient as each person grows.

Ministry

In supporting the vowed life, community living provides an environment that is meant to sustain and nourish religious men and women as they follow Jesus' command, "Go therefore and make disciples of all nations, baptizing them in the name of the Father and of the Son and of the Holy Spirit, and teaching them to obey everything that I have commanded you" (Matt 28:19-20). Religious life is a life of service. The "yes" of consecrated religious to follow Jesus through the vows lived in community leads them to a life of dedicated ministry. Using their individual gifts and talents, in concert with their congregation's mission, religious seek to serve God's people. The Constitutions of the Sisters of Saint Joseph describe the sisters as living and working so that all people may be united with God and with one another. That is the mission or reason for being of the congregation.[10] Their ministries then follow this mission and are meant to provide concrete ways to live out this mission.

Religious men and women perform good works, expressed through the spirit and mission of their congregation. They assist poor and marginalized persons, minister in parishes and schools, serve in soup kitchens and prisons, interact with youth and young adults, work in diocesan offices, and travel to mission lands near and far. One can see that education, social service, health care, and pastoral and spiritual ministries enable those called to this life to engage in all the spiritual and corporal works of mercy. Through these ministries, as far as they are able, religious bring the face of Christ to others in their daily service. Nobel Prize winner Albert Schweitzer, in addressing a group of students in the United States, observed, "I do not know what your destiny will be, but one thing I know; the only ones among you who will really be happy are those who have sought and found how to serve."[11] Ministry provides a way for religious men and women to use their gifts, channel their passion, and offer their time and talent in service. In return, ministry can foster deep joy and a profound sense of meaning while meeting the great needs within our world.

Prayer

Prayer is another significant aspect of religious life. It is the mortar that holds the life together and supports every part of religious life itself. People often think that priests, brothers, and sisters pray all day. This statement is true and yet not. In accordance with Saint Paul's request, "Pray in the Spirit at all times" (Eph 6:18), some religious men and women truly are contemplative and mark each of the hours of the day with prayer. Many, however, are active, apostolic religious so that while they root themselves in prayer that impels them outward in service to others and then sends them back again to prayer, they do not find themselves marking the hours with prayer like the contemplative cloistered religious. Each day all religious consecrate a period of time sufficiently long for personal, private prayer. They also share in communal prayer, usually in the morning and evening within the smaller community in which they live. Religious also participate in Eucharist, make an annual retreat, and nourish their prayer through spiritual reading. Prayer truly is the cornerstone of the consecrated religious life and makes all things possible in God.

The Call

Given the above-mentioned aspects of religious life and the unique promises of the vows, one might wonder who would be called to such a life and how they would know. Scripture confirms that anyone can be called! Look at Abraham, who thought he was too old but eventually left his homeland and became the

father of faith to many. Moses complained that he didn't have
the gift of speech, and God provided a spokesperson in Aaron.
Jeremiah thought he was too young, and God reassured him that
he would be with him to give him the words to speak. Isaiah
cried that he was a person of unclean lips living among a people
of unclean lips. God touched his mouth so that his wickedness
and sin would be removed. Ruth was a foreigner from a strange
land whose journey led her to become the ancestor of David and
of Jesus. Mary, while engaged to Joseph, questioned the angel
about how it could be possible that she would be the mother of
God, and her cousin, Elizabeth, who was to give birth to John
the Baptist, clearly knew that she was beyond the childbearing
years. Both women were carriers of God's chosen ones.

These biblical stories make it clear that life is never the same
once a person is called. These biblical figures leave what is familiar to them and know that new allegiances are expected. It
is clear that each vocation is a unique mystery. It's our story.
People commonly expect the call to be dramatic, clear, and un-
questionable. More times than not, it breaks into life when we
least expect it. It occurs in the midst of everyday, ordinary circumstances. It requires attention, prayer, patience, and docility
to the Holy Spirit. "Response to God's call is not an instantaneous or static reality but one that unfolds over time and one
that must endure the rigors of the march to Jerusalem, a journey
that often involves challenge, fatigue, and failure. Each one of
us has received a call. Our biblical heritage gives us the means
to understand that call and to respond in faith."[12] Those who are
called respond in freedom, and God reassures them that they
will have what they need to follow this call and that God will
accompany them on the journey.

While God calls all people to a life of holiness, God calls some
specifically to a vowed life as a religious priest, brother, or sister.
It is important to recognize that God calls in an infinite variety
of ways. God works through our unique personality and temperament. While there are no two identical ways in which God
calls, there are similarities and examples that describe how God
reaches us.

Sometimes there is a defining moment when people come to an awareness that turns their life around and points them to following Jesus more closely. They might describe their experience as a conversion, a turning toward Jesus. Often there is a recurring sense of wanting to follow Jesus in a life of service, but whenever this thought crosses their mind, they can easily dismiss it thinking "not me" or "I'm not good enough." Others experience a sense of wanting "more" and desiring to be satisfied on a deeper level than what the culture offers. It appears as if something is missing. Religious life, an alternative way of life, seems attractive and desirable as a more radical and deeply spiritual way of life. A person comes to recognize on a very personal level Saint Augustine's testimony, articulated in his *Confessions*, "You have made us for yourself, Lord, and our hearts are restless until they rest in you."[13] Still others observe that they are more energized and vital in their service or volunteer work than in their careers. Using their gifts and talents for the good of all captures their hearts, and sharing from the fruits of their relationship with God proves to be life-giving and life-sustaining. These are just some of the ways that God works in getting people's attention and inviting men and women to follow as vowed religious. Throughout this process, God always respects our freedom.

Discernment

The process of discernment helps one to figure out what God really desires so that one may respond in faith. It's a process and it takes time, prayer, and faithfulness. St. Ignatius of Loyola offered some time-tested guidelines for the discernment of spirits to help people discover what God is calling them to in all the decisions of their lives, especially vocational discernment. Father Warren Sazama, SJ, provides a practical vocation guide that outlines seven attitudes or qualities required for an authentic discernment process and seven steps to making sound, prayerful life decisions.

Openness entails both an open mind and an open heart so that one does not enter into the decision-making process with attachments, that is, limits or conditions on the freedom necessary to respond to God's will. *Generosity* allows a largeness of heart that puts no limits on what God calls a person to. Sazama says it is like writing God a signed blank check, letting God fill in the amount and content of the check! *Courage* enables one to respond to that to which God calls even if it might be challenging, difficult, or risky. It means letting go of control and trusting God implicitly. *Interior freedom* disposes people so that their whole and deepest desire is to do whatever God's will is for them with no conditions attached. This attitude directly contrasts with those who are all talk and no action. Such people become so distracted with their busyness that they never get around to what really matters: God's will for them. Or the opposite might be true. They do everything but the one thing necessary, the endeavor to which God is calling them. The habit of *prayerful reflection* on one's experience is essential since one cannot know that to which God is calling if one does not listen. And how can people listen if they do not pray and get in touch with the interior movements of their hearts? *Having one's priorities straight* puts everything else in life in the subordinate position of a means to the end, which is the ultimate goal of life—to serve God. Finally, *not confusing ends with means* rightfully puts God first in one's life and lets all other things follow. Sazama suggests that when individuals have these attitudes, then they have their satellite dish pointed in the right direction in order to receive God's signal. Possessing these qualities is the precondition for hearing God's call through an authentic discernment process.[14]

The seven steps to a good decision that Sazama identifies are quite helpful. First, discerners put priorities in order, keeping before themselves the purpose for which God created them. Second, they pray, paying attention to inner desires, and enter into spiritual direction. Third, they consider the options and explore the various lifestyles, careers, and communities to which they are attracted. Fourth, they explore personal experiences with the options to which they are drawn and with which they identify most closely. Fifth, the discerner gets a feel for which option is the best fit, providing a sense of belonging and offering the best opportunity for them to serve. Sixth, they make a decision recognizing that deciding entails a leap of faith and trust that they are in God's caring hands. Finally, once they make a decision, they look to see if God blesses them with a sense of inner peace and "rightness" over time. They watch for confirmation of their decision.[15]

Intrinsic to the call to follow Jesus is yet another call and that is to a particular community. Once discerners have surrendered to God's call then they must determine if they will become a Benedictine, a Franciscan, a Jesuit, a Sister of St. Joseph, a Carmelite, a Sister of the Immaculate Heart of Mary or a member of one of the many other religious communities that exist. It might be likened to finding a "home away from home." After all, if people are going to leave the comfort and safety of home then they want to find a place where they can equally be at home. Practically speaking, it is helpful to identify what people are looking for, that is, what fits best given one's personality, temperament, gifts, likes, and dislikes, as well as the kind of service that a person hopes to offer. For example, is a community that is larger or smaller in size more attractive? Does it matter if the community is local or international? Does the community involve itself in a variety of ministries or have a particular focus like health care or education? How do they pray and what is community life like? It is important for discerners to identify priorities and to look for a religious community where they can best be themselves. One note of caution—there is no perfect community!

A very critical aspect of this search to discover which community a person will belong to is not only information gathering but also visiting and spending time. Ultimately, it is important that this community be a place where a person can love and be loved, work by sharing personal talents and gifts in service, and grow in relationship with God. In discovering the community in which one will live out this call, there is a mutual discernment that is going on. The community is looking at the individual for a good fit just as the individual is looking at the community. It marks the beginning of a very mutual relationship with a community.

Formation

Eventually a person gets to a point where the discernment leads them to a decision of knowing, as far as possible, that one must literally "come and see." They realize that they are ready to begin a process of formation that will continue their discernment while living with religious in order to learn the life of those called to be a religious priest, brother, or sister. Once inquirers have discerned the call to join a religious community, they formally begin a process designed by the particular congregation and in keeping with required church law. While the titles for these various stages may vary among congregations, essentially the dynamic of the stages of formation is similar.

Initially, one becomes a candidate or postulant and has the opportunity to enjoy the hospitality and relationship of community members. One meets regularly with the formation director and engages in prayer, study, and discussion. The focus is to deepen the Christian commitment and to grow in a life of prayer and service. It is important that spiritual direction continue in this process as well. During this time, or at least part of this time, one lives with members of the community sharing in prayer and community living. At this stage, candidates might continue working in a ministry in which they are already involved, begin working in a new ministry, or engage in studies.

As a novice, the focus is on deepening one's relationship with Jesus Christ. A novice continues to discern the call to religious life, seeking greater self-knowledge, insight, and awareness of the presence of God. Solitude defines the novitiate experience and includes a balance of prayer, study, and ministry. Without a doubt, it is a unique period of time that calls for serious interior work that allows the novice to be rooted in the person God calls them to be, to know the congregation that they are becoming a member of, and to relate intimately to Jesus Christ to whom they are committing their life. At the end of this period of discernment, if a novice expresses the desire to continue with the process of formation and the congregation confirms this desire then the novice makes first profession of vows. Depending on the congregation's constitutions, religious renew those vows yearly or for two or three years at a time until they make final profession.

As an initially professed religious, one deepens and celebrates the commitment to Jesus Christ through the renewal of vows. During this time, one is fully involved in the work of the congregation and continues to gather regularly for days of prayer, study, spiritual guidance, and instruction in the essentials of religious life. Through the act of perpetual profession, a religious man or woman publicly confirms the desire to love God and others and to live in vowed membership throughout a lifetime.

When all is said and done regarding discerning a call to religious life, the individual must trust. God invites each person to step out in faith even though one cannot see the end, only the horizon that lies ahead. So with a long line of predecessors, Jesus calls each to follow. There is the testimony of countless vowed religious over many, many years that the loving God who created them and provided for them all along the way will not abandon them now. So take heart in this powerfully profound and personal message that God is with each person on the journey.

If you ever visit Chicago, you must see the sculpture *Cloud Gate* located in Millennium Park. It is one of my favorite places to visit and to take others to see as well. It is mammoth, inspiring, and radiates greatness. Nicknamed *The Bean* because of its legume-like shape, this 110-ton elliptical sculpture is forged of a seamless series of highly polished stainless steel plates. The sculpture reflects the city's skyline and the clouds above. A twelve-foot-high arch provides a "gate" to the concave chamber beneath the sculpture, inviting visitors to touch its mirror-like surface and see their images reflected back from a variety of perspectives. Patrice Tuohy, publisher of *Vision*, the annual National Religious Vocation Conference discernment guide, has drawn a marvelous insight about this sculpture and discerning a vocation that I would like to pass on to you:

> Preeminent twentieth century architect Daniel Burnham advised his associates: "Make no little plans. They have no magic to stir

men's blood and probably will not themselves be realized."
His words inspired enormous risk-taking and talent-searching
from subsequent generations of city planners, architects, and
artists, including Anish Kapoor who created this sculpture.
Burnham's advice extends beyond the artist's call. All vocations have a public and personal impact. Entering religious life
is not only a decision between a person and God but between
that person and the community as well. Each person's call is a
call to service. As such, it is important to draw on the perspective and wisdom of others as one decides on a life course. Like
the panorama of "Cloud Gate," take in the big picture, look at
things from various angles and different points of view. Above
all make no little plans. Think of what one man from the dusty
town of Nazareth was able to accomplish. In following Jesus,
one is on the path to greatness, to holiness, to a life not without
its slings and arrows but filled with all-encompassing, excessive
love and mercy.[16]

May this insight and advice serve as a reminder that God has
great plans for you. The prophet Jeremiah reminds all of us, "For
surely I know the plans I have for you, says the LORD, plans for
your welfare and not for harm, to give you a future with hope"
(Jer 29:11). Trust these plans knowing that there is no harm in
discovering at any point along the journey that religious life
does not give you the greatest joy in being the person God is
calling you to be. The faithful pursuit has led you to greater self-
knowledge, deeper relationship with God, and much experience
filled with learning. There can be no regret in that discovery!

On a more personal note, I can remember some very simple
advice that my mother offered when I shared with her my desire
to become a vowed religious. In her very realistic and direct
manner, she cautioned me to remember that the convent would
be no different than life in the "real world." She continued by
noting that I would find a very real "slice of life" in the convent.
In other words, I wouldn't be relieved of dealing with difficult
personalities, hard missions, challenging ministries, disappointment, and disillusionment. However, she told me that when I
found myself in the midst of these realities that I should go to

my room, close my door, and speak to the Lord! At the time, her words were challenging to hear. As time has unfolded, I have deeply appreciated her wisdom. Jesus has truly become the absolute in my life. Religious life can really be a wonderful life for those whom God calls. It is not the life for everyone, and yet if it is the call, then one need not be afraid. Jesus reminds us in John's gospel, "I came that they may have life and have it abundantly" (John 10:10).

This chapter on religious life would be incomplete if it did not include one more consideration—the climate of religious life in this twenty-first century. It is no secret that congregations today are dealing with fewer sisters, brothers, and priests. This diminishment causes concern when it is compared to the largest numbers of religious men and women reached by 1965. I have always regarded those years when large numbers of men and women entered religious life as the blip on the screen. In other words, that phenomenon was unusual and yet it has become the norm to which we compare the reality of religious life today. If this life is a call from God, a true following of Jesus and a countercultural lifestyle, it cannot be meant for the multitudes. So those who choose to respond to God's call today are entering communities that are in the process of trying to respond to this reality in a way that is life-giving and faithful to their mission. There is no doubt that religious life is in the midst of change and this is an important awareness for people to have as they look to throwing their lot in with others in a religious community.

I like to believe that this time in religious life is a time of renewal and rebirth. No doubt, God is creating something new and we are only beginning to perceive it. Like any change it requires letting go. It may even cost deeply. And most important, it requires a desire and willingness to discern how God is inviting those in religious life at this time to become what is needed in the church and in the world. We cannot overlook the significance and power of God's call in those whom God chooses at this time. It is no coincidence or accident that God calls them at this time and especially at this time in the history of a given congregation. Religious life needs the vitality, vision, energy, and passion, as well as the gifts and talents of those whom God is calling today. Indeed, God is still calling people and God may very well be calling you. Consider the invitation in the lyrics of the song, "The Summons":

> Will you come and follow me if I but call your name?
> Will you go where you don't know and never be the same?
> Will you let my love be shown, will you let my name
>   be known,
> will you let my life be grown in you and you in me?
> Lord, your summons echoes true when you but call
>   my name.
> Let me turn and follow you and never be the same.
> In your company I'll go where your love and footsteps show.
> Thus I'll move and live and grow in you and you in me.[17]

Will you take up the challenge and follow the call? Will you respond?

For Reflection

- How has God's loving activity been present in your life?
- What would it be like to commit yourself to a life of service?
- What do you see as the joys and challenges of life as a religious brother, sister, or priest?
- How do you understand community living and why is it important to you?
- What encourages you to move forward in undertaking a vocational discernment? What holds you back?
- What is your/God's desire for your "one wild and precious life" and how has God entrusted and gifted you for that life?

Scripture Passages

Psalm 139	Jeremiah 29:11-15	Mark 1:16-20
Mark 10:17-22	John 1:35-42	Romans 12:1-2

Recommended Reading

Mack, John P., Jr. *Priests: An Inside Look*. Winona, MN: Saint Mary's Press, 2001.

Martin, James. *Becoming Who You Are: Insights on the True Self from Thomas Merton and Other Saints*. Mahwah, NJ: Paulist Press, 2006.

————. *In Good Company: The Fast Track from the Corporate World to Poverty, Chastity, and Obedience*. Lanham, MD: Rowman & Littlefield, 2000.

————. *My Life With the Saints*. Chicago, IL: Loyola Press, 2006.

Palmer, Parker J. *Let Your Life Speak: Listening for the Voice of Vocation*. San Francisco, CA: Jossey-Bass, 2000.

Rooney, Kathleen. *Sisters: An Inside Look*. Winona, MN: Saint Mary's Press, 2000.

Schatz, Larry. *Brothers: An Inside Look*. Winona, MN: Saint Mary's Press, 2002.

Silf, Margaret. *Inner Compass: An Invitation to Ignatian Spirituality*. Chicago, IL: Loyola Press, 1999.

VISION: The Annual Religious Vocation Discernment Guide. Chicago, IL: TrueQuest Communications, 2009.

8

Stephen Bevans, SVD

A Ministry for Ministry: The Vocation of Ministerial Priesthood in the Church

A Sacrament of Service and Vocation

The *Catechism of the Catholic Church* (CCC) designates two of our seven sacraments as sacraments of service. "They confer a particular mission in the Church and serve to build up the People of God" (1534). These two sacraments have also been called "sacraments of vocation," because while they certainly are for the benefit of those who receive and live them out in their lives, they are really more for the benefit of *others*.

The first of these, the sacrament of matrimony or marriage, besides being a source of God's grace for an individual couple, also serves the church and the world by being a living sign of God's love in Christ for all humanity. A husband and wife give themselves completely to one another, sacrifice for one another, grow with one another, love one another "for richer, for poorer, in sickness and in health" for their entire lives in a union that cannot be broken. When they really do that, they demonstrate in their daily lives how God in Christ has given and continues to give his whole self to men and women, and will never abandon them no matter what they do—even if they turn away.

Naturally, God's love and fidelity is infinitely greater than any love human beings can have for one another, but the wonder is that human love can actually point to that love in a small but truly accurate way. In a world that is scarred by divorce, infidelity, and abusive relationships, the faithful love of a married couple is actually a prophetic sign of God's faithfulness and healing presence in the lives of human beings.

The second of the sacraments of service and vocation is the sacrament of holy order[1] or ordained ministry. A bishop's, priest's, or deacon's life of pastoral leadership in the church, if lived consciously and well, is a sign of *Christ's* leadership in the church as prophet, priest, and servant leader. Christ alone, as the Scriptures say, is "head of the body, the church" (Col 1:18). But in the same way that married couples can be signs of God's love, those who are ordained can also be signs of Christ's prophetic and priestly leadership. The pope is not the head of the church, the bishop is not the head of a diocese, the priest is not the head of the parish: Christ is! Nevertheless, some members of the church are entrusted with that leadership, as fragile as they are.

This present chapter will reflect on the second of these sacraments of service and vocation, the sacrament of holy order, and in particular it will reflect on the ordained or ministerial priesthood. As the title of this chapter indicates, priesthood is a "ministry for ministry." It is not an end in itself, but a ministry in the church that has the task—indeed, the *privilege*—of calling God's people to their full potential as members of the Body of Christ and as the Temple of the Holy Spirit.

Priesthood is a vocation that, in today's world, is a costly one. It usually demands lifelong celibacy and the development of a high level of pastoral skills. Today—in the wake of the sexual abuse crisis of the last decade and in the context of an increasingly consumerist and individualist culture—priesthood seems to be a vocation that is no longer a highly desired one. Especially in the United States and other developed countries, there is a serious shortage of priests that probably won't get any less serious in the foreseeable future.

Because, though, of its importance in the church and in the world and because too of the incredible privilege of being a sacrament of Christ's presence and leadership, ordained ministry is a vocation that every Catholic person who qualifies should at least consider.[2]

A Vocation within the Church

Important for understanding ordained ministry and ministerial priesthood today is to realize that it is a sacrament of vocation *within the church*. To say this implies two things. First, the priest is not a super-Christian but a person who shares with his sisters and brothers in the church the common call to be Christian that is rooted in his baptism. Second, priesthood is a ministry, a life lived in service for the sake of the church and its mission.

Vatican II's teaching on priesthood and several subsequent official documents[3] make a point that ordained ministry is a ministry altogether different from the ministry of other Christians—it does not differ in *degree* but in essence (LG 10; PDV 17). We'll speak about that difference a bit later in this reflection, but let's now focus on what ministerial priests have in common with all other Christians.

Even though his specific ministry is a *different* ministry than the ministry other Christians share, a priest still lives his Christianity out of his dedication to God in baptism, a dedication that is sealed in the sacrament of confirmation and celebrated and renewed in the Eucharist. As the *Catechism of the Catholic Church* puts it, these three sacraments "ground the common vocation of all Christ's disciples, a vocation to holiness and to the mission of evangelizing the world" (1533).

What this statement means is that, in the first place, every Christian is called to continue Jesus' *prophetic* ministry by living a life of witness to the gospel and, when appropriate and necessary, proclaiming her or his faith in words. Such a prophetic ministry may also be expressed by Christians as they read the

Scriptures in liturgical celebrations and, at appropriate times, break open the Word for the assembled Christian community. Second, the sentence from the *Catechism* quoted above means that every Christian shares the *priestly* ministry of Christ by living a life of integrity, sacrifice, and love (see Rom 12:1) and joining the Christian community in offering the sacrifice of praise of the Eucharist. Third, to speak of the "common vocation of all Christ's disciples" means that each Christian is called to continue Jesus' ministry of *service* by serving the church and the world in some kind of way. Grace is never for oneself. It is always for the sake of others. Every baptized Christian is called to live a life of service, whether as a loving and sacrificing parent, an honest employee, or more formally in a recognized form of ministry in the Christian community like lectoring, bringing Communion to the sick, teaching children about the faith, directing a choir, or serving on the staff of a retreat house or parish.

There exists, then, a fundamental equality and dignity of all Christians because of their baptism (see LG 31–32). While some ministries demand more responsibility from Christians, each ministry is of equal importance within the entire church. St. Augustine said this well when he said that while he was a bishop *for* the community, *with* the community he was still a Christian: "What I am for you terrifies me; what I am with you consoles me. . . . The former is a duty; the latter a grace. The former is a danger; the latter, salvation."[4]

So like all Christians, a priest is called to service. As the U.S. bishops said it some three decades ago, a priest is "one [among many] who serves."[5] This is an important point, because priestly office is also a position of leadership, authority, and power. The priest, as Pope John Paul II puts it, is "not only in the Church but also in the forefront of the Church" (PDV 16). Priests must be careful to interpret their power, however, in *Christian* terms, and not in the way of earthly kings (see Luke 22:25). Referring to the way in which earthly rulers lord their authority over others, Jesus told his disciples, "But not so with you; rather the greatest among you must become like the youngest, and the leader like one who serves" (Luke 22:26).

Through the ages, ordained ministers gradually assumed power and authority in the church to such an extent that those who were not ordained—the laity—were reduced to passive members of the church. Reasons for this were complex and in certain circumstances were fully justified. The result, however, was that ordained ministry was often regarded as a life of power and privilege. Laypeople who wanted to participate more fully in the church's ministry were regarded with suspicion, because it was said that their only functions in the church were to "pay, pray, and obey."

Today, as priests recognize their unity with all God's people, they realize that such exclusive exercise of power is out of place. There are certainly still pastors who make unilateral decisions and abuse their position in the church, but we know that this is hardly the ideal. Those who hold authority and power in the church are rather called to use that power in service. Being in the "forefront of the church" is not to be a position of prestige and honor, but a position of responsibility. It is a position of service to the entire church community.

The Service of Ordering

Just what such service is leads us back to the question of the uniqueness of priestly identity—how the ministerial priesthood is an entirely different ministry from other ministries in the church. The difference is this: while all Christians (including those ordained) are called to participate in Jesus' prophetic, priestly, and servant ministry within the church and in the world, those who are ordained to *ministerial* priesthood are called to lead, coordinate, foster, train, and regulate the life of the church. They are called to a *ministry for ministry*.

Another way to think about this altogether different ministry of ordained ministers in the church is to make a kind of word-play on the name of the sacrament that commissions them for this ministry: the sacrament of holy order. Originally, of course, the sacrament referred to the rite by which Christians were commissioned (ordained) for a particular *order* in the church: the order of bishop, priest, or deacon (CCC 1537). But what if we made "order" into a verb? What if we spoke about the sacrament of holy *ordering*? This would point clearly to the unique ministry that ordained Christians fulfill in the church: the *ordering* of the Christian community. We could then speak about the fact that the task of ordained ministry, ministerial priesthood, is to *order* the Christian community, to work for the holy order of the Christian community, so that the Christian community can more effectively work for *God's* holy order in the world, what we also call the reign of God.

Again, this is only a wordplay. But it does help us understand what ordained ministry is all about. We can further speak about how this ordering is threefold. The ministry of the priest is that of ordering the church's *prophetic* ministry, ordering the church's *priestly* ministry, and ordering its *ministry of service* or the structure of its ministry.

First of all, the ministry of the priest is that of ordering the church's prophetic ministry, or working to guarantee that the faith witnessed to and professed by Christians in their lives is faithful to the original gospel that Jesus proclaimed to the apostolic church. There are all sorts of ways a priest does this: teaching adult education classes, doing baptismal and marriage preparation, giving retreats, for example. But the main way that an ordained minister fulfills this ministry of ordering the church's prophetic ministry and faith is by proclaiming and explaining the Word in the context of liturgical celebrations. Vatican II's document on priesthood, *Presbyterorum Ordinis* (PO), speaks of the fact that "it is the first task of priests as co-workers of the bishops to preach the Gospel of God to all" (4). The great challenge to priests today is the challenge of being good preachers, of opening the Scriptures in ways that people can understand and be challenged, of bringing the good news of the gospel into the everyday lives of people so that they can live it more faithfully in their families and on their jobs.

This is a pastoral skill that takes a lot of hard work to develop to its full potential, and one never stops learning and growing in this area. Someone who is discerning whether he has a vocation to the priesthood needs to discern whether he has a passion for God's Word, and a passion for communicating it to ordinary men and women. If not, ministerial priesthood is probably not for him. There are persons, though, who are called to preach. They have the gift of the turn of a phrase, the ability to tell a story. They possess insight into the foibles and beauty of life, and a desire to study the Scriptures. For such persons priesthood might just be something to which God is calling them.

The second aspect of priestly ministry is the task of ordering the church's priestly ministry. As the Scriptures and the early theologians of the church knew well, all Christians share equally in Christ's priesthood. It was only in the Middle Ages that the priesthood of all believers was eclipsed by the ordained priesthood, but this great doctrine has been recovered again by Vatican II. Again, there are several ways that the ministerial priest can fulfill this ministry—for example in spiritual direction—but the main way that this ministry is carried out is through the priest's presiding at celebrations of the liturgy.

Note that the word is *preside*. The priest, technically, is never the *celebrant* of a liturgy. That is the ministry of all Christians present, since all Christians are priestly people. The priest presides in the sense that he *orders* the celebration. He is the one who coordinates the various ministries in liturgy: readers, greeters, cantors, extraordinary ministers of Communion, etc. He is the one who speaks in the name of Christ and of the community at the eucharistic prayer, or in the giving of absolution, or anointing, or baptism. He is the one who by his prayerful manner and inclusive attitude inspires all the celebrants of the liturgy to deeper prayer. Presiding is an art. It is an acquired skill. And yet, as the saying goes, grace builds on nature. Some people just have the flair, the poise, the presence. Someone discerning a call to priesthood should ask himself whether he has such talent, but—maybe more important—whether he has the passion to lead a community in prayer and celebration.

A third way that the priest serves the holy order of the church is by ordering its *ministerial structure*, or being responsible for the development of ministers in the church. Ordained ministry in the church used to be practically the only way one could do ministry in the church, but this is not the case today. Today we understand the church in a way that is closer to a New Testament understanding of the church, with many ministers and many ministries working together for the building up of the entire church body. And so the task of the priest today is to call for women and men in the Christian community to discern their own calls to ministry. His task is further to discern among his community members who indeed would make effective and fruitful ministers of the Word, ministers of the Eucharist, ministers who might take care of finances, who could visit the sick, who have the talent to enhance liturgies by music ministry, who can participate in marriage and baptismal preparation—and many more such ministries.

The priest's task is to make sure that these women and men are well trained in their ministry, that they have continuing education in ministry, and that they reflect together on their ministerial experiences in the light of God's Word and the Christian tradition. He might also have to admonish and correct ministers who make mistakes, or even abuse their authority. Much of this also might be delegated to other ministers whose job it is to train, offer spiritual direction, lead support groups, or lead groups of theological reflection. Someone reflecting on whether he is called to the ministerial priesthood needs to ask himself if he is the kind of person who can discover the ministerial talents of others and empower and encourage them in ministry. No one can do all the church's ministry, not in today's church. Only a person who thrives on real collaboration is one who is fit to take on priestly ministry.

Images of Priesthood

One powerful image of the ministerial priest today, as he serves the community by ordering it, is that of the conductor of an orchestra. As the conductor does not play every instrument in the orchestra, but coordinates the tempo, the blend, the loudness and softness of the music, the "feel" of the music, so the priest does not perform every ministry, but coordinates the entire community. His is an indispensable job, for without the wisdom and the authority of the conductor the orchestra cannot play to its full potential. But his is a ministry that is largely one that is more subtle, indirect, inspirational. This of course does not mean that the ministerial priest does not do hands-on ministry; certainly presiding over liturgical celebrations, preaching, doing spiritual direction, and the like are ministries in which he engages. But all of these include a way of doing ministry that is formative of the Christian community, calling forth the potential of the community. In the inspiring words of John Paul II, the ministry of the priest is to "help the People of God to exercise faithfully and fully the common priesthood which it has received" (PDV 17).

Another image that might help us understand the service of ordering that is the specific ministry of ordained priests is an ancient one and takes us to the heart of the theology of the sacrament. This is the image of supervision or oversight. Such an image is at the heart of the theology of the sacrament of holy order because these words are translations of the Greek *episkopē*, which reflects the Greek word *episkopos* that we now translate "bishop." Ultimately, the fullness of the sacrament of holy order resides in the ministry of the bishop, whose task is to supervise or oversee (*episkopein*) the entire Christian community, making sure it professes the faith of the apostolic church, that it celebrates the liturgy worthily, that it is a living community of ministers, and that it is continuing Jesus' mission of service to God's holy order, the reign of God. Priestly ministry shares in episcopal ministry, overseeing a particular Christian community in the bishop's name, in terms of the bishop's prophetic (preaching), liturgical, and governing leadership. Diaconal ministry shares in episcopal ministry especially in terms of the bishop's duty to oversee the church's ministry of charity and justice, but also to a certain extent in the bishop's prophetic and liturgical leadership as well. Once more, ministry is the task of the entire church. The bishop's, priest's, and deacon's ministry is to make sure that that ministry is activated and developed.

Conformed to Christ the Head

A further, and perhaps more "ontological," approach to understanding the unique way that ordained ministry differs from the ministry shared by all Christians is to speak of priests as conformed to Christ the head of the Body, the church. This image goes back to Paul's powerful insight that Christians share such intimacy with Christ through baptism and participation in the Eucharist that they can be said to be "one body" with him, and so literally continue Christ's mission on earth (see Gal 3:27-28; Rom 6:3-11; 1 Cor 10:6-7). In Romans 12 and First Corinthians 12, Paul also speaks of the church as Christ's body, and how each member's gifts are similar to the various parts of the body, which need to work in harmony with one another if the body is to flourish. Building on this imagery, the authors of the letters to the Ephesians and Colossians extend the imagery to a reflection on the fact that if the church is indeed the Body of Christ, it nevertheless does not thereby *control* Christ. Rather, Christ is the *head* of the Body, the church, and so is the one ultimately guiding and governing the church, not the human leaders of the community or the church itself (see Eph 1:22-23; Col 1:13-20; 2:16-19).

In the same way, as Vatican II expresses it and as it is echoed in the writings of John Paul II, we can speak of the church as the Body of Christ, continuing his threefold mission of prophecy, priesthood, and servanthood, but we can also speak of the ordained minister as being a sacrament of Christ's headship of the church (see PO 2, 6; PDV 4, 12, 13). As we have said before, no human being is *actually* the head of the church—not even the pope. But in order that the holy order of the church may be served so that the church may faithfully serve the world, there exist in the church *sacraments* of Christ's headship, and this is the identity of ordained ministry in the church.

John Paul II speaks of ordained ministers as conformed to Christ the *shepherd* and *spouse* of the church as well. These deeply scriptural images (e.g., John 10; Eph 5) are powerful. It should be noted, however, that they are not so much images of *privilege* (although such conformity to Christ is indeed an ineffable privilege!) as they are images of responsibility and ministry. Sacraments always confer a grace and a task. The specific task of the ordained or ministerial priest is to live up to what he has become through the sacrament: a living sign of Christ the head of the Body, the shepherd of the church, the spouse of the church. In his earthly ministry, Jesus did not cling to any privilege (see Phil 2:9) but came to serve (see Mark 10:45).

The best image of Jesus' ministry, and our own, is perhaps that of John 13, the passage that describes Jesus washing the feet of the disciples: "After he had washed their feet, had put on his robe, and had returned to the table, he said to them, 'Do you know what I have done to you? You call me Teacher and Lord—and you are right, for that is what I am. So if I, your Lord and Teacher, have washed your feet, you also ought to wash one another's feet. For I have set you an example, that you also should do as I have done to you'" (John 13:12-15).

It is conformity to this exercise of power and authority of Jesus' leadership that helps us understand how the ordained minister is conformed to Christ the head, shepherd, and spouse of the church.

Models of Ministerial Priesthood

No one way of describing ministerial priesthood is completely adequate. We have been describing priestly ministry as a "ministry for ministers," or what some writers have called the model of "pastoral leadership." There are, though, other possible ways of explaining priestly ministry. After all, this is a ministry that is so rich that no one way of talking about it can exhaust its meaning.

A number of years ago the late Avery Dulles (before he was a cardinal) outlined four models of ministerial priesthood.[6] These models might be helpful for understanding the model that we are proposing here. A first model that Dulles proposes is that of the priest as servant of the Word. This is a model, he says, that focuses on the priest's duty to preach and proclaim the Word, which, as we have seen, is described by Vatican II as his "first task" (PO 4). In second place, Dulles proposes the model of the priest as the dispenser of the sacraments. Ultimately, he says, this is the model advocated by Pope John Paul II in his various writings, and it focuses on the priest's liturgical role. The third model Dulles lays out is that of pastoral leader, a model we will return to shortly. Dulles's own preferred model, however, is that of the priest as representative of Christ. In a way that is irrevocable, the priest is marked with the identity of Christ and represents him within the church and in the world outside the church as well. The great advantage of this model, Dulles suggests, is that the identity of the priest does not depend on anything he *does*, but on what he *is* or *has become*.

Any of these models is adequate for an understanding of the identity of the priest today, especially if it is not taken as the *exclusive* model. What commends the model of pastoral leader, however, as compared to the other three, is that this model is in itself an inclusive one. The way that we have been describing the priest's identity emphasizes his leadership in the proclamation of the Word, in the celebration of the liturgy and the sacraments, and also points to the basis for such leadership: the priest's conformity to Christ the head and leader of the church. The image also has the advantage of being able to acknowledge in a clear way the call of ministry of every Christian, the service of which is the priest's task as pastoral leader and sacrament of Christ.

There is no doubt, however, that each priest, whether diocesan or religious, will gravitate to one of these models according to his own theological perspective and personal gifts. Some priests will excel in preaching, others in inspiring a community's ministry, and still others in liturgical presidency. Some religious congregations of men will cultivate a particular style of priesthood according to their own charism and their character as religious in the church. Redemptorists and Passionists, for example, might emphasize the service of the Word; Benedictines and Norbertines might emphasize skill at liturgical presiding; Jesuits might focus on how even in teaching secular subjects they represent Christ in a particularly distinct way; missionary congregations such as the Society of the Divine Word, the Columbans, or Maryknoll might emphasize the pastoral leadership model as they form local churches and call forth local leadership in cross-cultural situations.

Most important, however, is that any image or model of ministerial priesthood today be one that is a "ministry for ministry." Being a sacrament of Christ's leadership in the church is always to call forth the potential of the whole church, and not keep ministry to oneself. Ministry belongs to the church. Ministerial priesthood serves that ministry.

A Twofold Vocation

The ministerial priesthood, as we said at the beginning of this chapter, is a vocation that every qualified Catholic should at least consider as he discerns his vocation in life. As necessary as it is in the church, and as exalted a state that is, it is not an easy life, and certainly not as prestigious as it once was in the church. And yet, it may well be that God in the Spirit is calling a person to embrace such a life of leadership and service to God's prophetic, priestly, and servant people. For many, a call to the priesthood might very well connect a person's deepest gladness with the deepest hungers of the world, as Frederick Buechner so famously described a vocation.[7]

Still, it is important to stress the fact that a vocation to the ministerial priesthood is not a private affair, something between only God and the person who is called. Since the ministerial priesthood is a vocation that serves the church community, it is the church community that ultimately must call a person to serve in that capacity. It is only after the person has been chosen by the church that the church can admit him to ordination into the sacrament of holy order. We see this played out in the ordination rite itself, when only after it has been testified that the person is worthy to be ordained does the ordaining bishop begin the ordination ceremony. Unlike after the sacrament of baptism, when every Christian has a *right* to do some kind of ministry in the church, no one has a right to be ordained. It is not something one takes upon himself. It is a ministry that is conferred upon him by the church.

Who Would Want to Become a Priest?
What Kind of Person Would the Church Choose?

Serving the church as a "minister for ministers" is not for everybody. Such a person would have to be someone who has a natural penchant for leadership, but who understands leadership as calling for the gifts of others. He would have to be a person of authority in the original sense of the word: helping women and men *author* their own lives and their own talents for service. A person discerning his vocation to the ministerial priesthood would have to recognize in himself a person who can preside with grace and prayerfulness, a person of wisdom who can open up new dimensions in God's Word as it is proclaimed, a person who can help Christians cherish their two-thousand-year-old tradition. A person discerning a vocation to the priesthood would have to recognize in himself a desire to keep growing in knowledge and in spirituality—as he enters into formal priestly formation and as he commits himself to continual education and formation after ordination. He would have to have a sense of self-denial, able to handle the rigors of a celibate life. And yet he would be a person who loves people, who wants to journey with them and share some of the most intimate moments of their lives. He would have to be a person who is able to cultivate deep and rich relationships with both women and men. There would have to be a deep sense of the equality of all Christians, of Christians' right to ministry in the church.

All this should be grounded, of course, in a deep faith and relationship to the God who is present at all times and places through the Spirit and who has manifested God's self concretely in the historical person of Jesus of Nazareth. Ultimately, in fact, it is God's grace that makes a priest a sacrament of God's presence in the church and in the world, not any qualities that a person has in himself. Grace builds on nature, but in the end it is indeed *grace* that builds. Catholics need to be *on call*. They need to be open to the possibility that they may be called to the ministerial priesthood. But it is always God who does the calling.

For Reflection

- Have you ever seriously considered a call to the ministerial priesthood? Why or why not?
- What do you think is the most important aspect of priestly ministry?
- What do you think makes priestly ministry different from other ministries in the church?
- Think of some of the priests you have known in your life. What qualities have made them effective ministers? What qualities have made them ineffective?
- What are some aspects of your own personality and talents that might make you a candidate for ministerial priesthood?
- What are the reasons why you might consider ministerial priesthood as a vocation in the church? What are the reasons why you might not consider it?

Scripture Passages

Matthew 10:37-39	Mark 9:33-37	Luke 22:24-27
John 13:1-15	1 Corinthians 12	Ephesians 4:11-16

Recommended Reading

Brown, Raymond. *Priest and Bishop: Biblical Reflections*. New York: Paulist Press, 1970.

Catechism of the Catholic Church, Part Two, Section Two, Chapter 3, Article 6, "The Sacrament of Holy Orders," paragraphs 1536–1600.

Confoy, Maryanne. *Religious Life and Priesthood: Perfectae Caritatis, Optatam Totius, Presbyterorum Ordinis*. Mahwah, NJ: Paulist Press, 2008.

Dulles, Avery. "Models of Ministerial Priesthood," *Origins* 20 (1990): 284–89.

John Paul II, Apostolic Exhortation, *I Will Give You Shepherds (Pastores Dabo Vobis)*.

Kasper, Walter Cardinal. *Leadership in the Church: How Traditional Roles Can Serve the Community Today*. New York: Crossroad, 2003.

Osborne, Kenan. *Orders and Ministry*. Maryknoll, NY: Orbis Books, 2006.

Smith, Karen Sue, ed. *Priesthood in the Modern World: A Reader*. Franklin, WI: Sheed and Ward, 1999.

United States Conference of Catholic Bishops. As One Who Serves. Washington, DC: United States Catholic Conference, 1977.

Vatican Council II, Decree on the Ministry and Life of Priests, *Presbyterorum Ordinis*.

Wood, Susan, ed. *Ordering the Baptismal Priesthood: Theologies of Lay and Ordained Ministry*. Collegeville, MN: Liturgical Press, 2003.

9

Robin Ryan, CP

Gathering the Fragments

The authors of this book offer important insights about the foundation, context, and dynamics of vocational discernment. The principles that are presented here flow from the rich tradition of Catholic theology and spirituality. These authors present their ideas not merely from their academic expertise but also from their personal experience as committed religious, priests, and lay ministers. The amount of information presented here may seem a bit overwhelming to women and men who are trying to sort through the possibilities of service in the church and make the best decisions for their lives. One may need to read these chapters more than once and take time to reflect on each of them as part of his or her discernment.

There are some salient themes that are found throughout these essays that are important for anyone who is discerning God's call. I will comment on these themes in this concluding chapter.

While we live in a culture of choice in North America, discerning one's vocation involves responding to a call. When he addressed the topic of culture and discipleship Robert Schreiter underlined the significance of the value of choice in the individualist culture of North America. As he put it, in our culture each person is expected to construct his or her own life. In his reflection on the biblical understanding of vocation, Donald Senior pointed out that in the New Testament the life of discipleship begins not with a choice but with a call. Choice and call are not completely opposite realities. When all is said and done, we have to make concrete choices in order to respond to God's call as we discern it in our lives. And as people of faith we believe that God respects and engages our freedom in the process of discernment. We should never think of ourselves as robots or slaves in our relationship with God. But this notion of call, which is so central to our biblical and spiritual heritage, alerts us to the challenge of self-transcendence in Christian discipleship. We must be willing to look beyond our immediate and more superficial desires and be open to what may be unfamiliar and challenging. Like Abraham and Sarah, we may be invited to journey to an unknown land. Responding to God's call entails ongoing conversion and personal transformation. Bishop Morneau said that discernment requires a listening heart and a passion to do God's will. To envision one's life as a response to a call is a countercultural stance. It is ultimately based on the gospel truth that when we are willing to lose our lives for Christ we find them again.

God's call to serve others comes to ordinary people. Donald Senior catalogued an intriguing cast of biblical characters, all of whom were convinced that they were not prepared for the mission that God was giving them: Abraham, Sarah, Moses, Isaiah, Jeremiah, Mary, and so forth. Through the ages great saints and leaders of the church have testified to feeling completely inadequate in their efforts to fulfill what God was asking of them. Nevertheless, they still managed to accomplish marvelous things. This theme brings us back to our discussion of the foundations of prayer, in which we saw that our life with God in all of its dimensions is dependent on God's grace. God gives of self to us so that we may know and love him, and God's indwelling presence empowers us to accomplish his will. Discerning one's call is a response to the love of God, who has loved us first and whose love for us always precedes and makes possible our response. The holy men and women of our tradition were able to be faithful to God's call in their lives because they were not relying merely on their own strength. They were empowered and transformed by divine grace—God's loving self-communication.

The search for God's will takes place within the Christian community. In his presentation on the church as communion Thomas Rausch began by reminding us that Catholicism is an essentially communal expression of Christian faith. We are invited to a shared life with God and with one another. Stephen Bevans pointed out that the call to priesthood is not a private affair but comes from the community. Sheila McLaughlin echoed this important principle, reminding us that vocational discernment is meant to happen within community, not in isolation. It is true that there is something eminently personal about discerning the path that one's life will take. It is a sacred choice that ultimately emerges from the sanctuary of one's conscience. But as members of a community of faith we believe that we are mediators of God's grace to one another. In making important decisions about our lives we need the insight, inspiration, and guidance that come from others within the Body of Christ. Making a decision about a vocation to lay ecclesial ministry, religious life, or priesthood requires an ongoing dialogue with the community, and it needs the approval of those who exercise authority in the church.

Finding peers who are also committed to discerning their vocation is a source of strength and encouragement for young adults. This observation is related, of course, to the need to discern one's call within the Christian community. As indicated in the first chapter of this book the young adults who attend Catholics on Call conferences consistently comment on their appreciation for the opportunity to meet and interact with like-minded peers who are on the same road of vocational discernment. They say that they sometimes feel very alone in searching for God's call in their lives. While speaking with older adults, especially trusted mentors, is important for discernment (see below), there is something very reassuring about meeting people one's own age who have similar dreams and aspirations. Dialoguing with other young adults who are thinking about a life of service in the church helps a person recognize that this is a realistic possibility for ordinary men and women. It is not a "strange" way of life.

One's peers also have a firsthand knowledge of the influences and pressures at work in the lives of young adults that impact the process of discernment. Young adult discerners need the mutual support, insight, and inspiration that come from gathering with their peers.

Discerning God's call requires a stance of listening. Listening is much more than hearing the words of others when they speak to us. At its deepest level listening involves the loving attention of which Bishop Morneau speaks. It entails a stance of openness and attentiveness toward others, God, oneself, and life in general. Listening demands self-discipline and self-transcendence. It often means moving beyond one's immediate needs and concerns—setting aside one's agenda—in order to be present to someone else. In discerning one's vocation, listening particularly involves attentiveness to the mysterious ways in which God addresses us. As the saints testify, so often God speaks to us through others, especially through those people to whom we entrust our hearts. We also need to cultivate the art of listening to ourselves, to our deepest desires. The spiritual masters of our tradition have taught us that knowledge of God and knowledge of self increase together. The stronger our friendship with God becomes the better we come to know ourselves. And the closer in touch we are with ourselves—with our gifts, struggles, and deepest desires—the more capable we are of discerning where God is leading us.

We need the help of wise, trustworthy mentors in discerning what God is asking of us. This is true not simply in deciding about the fundamental direction of one's life but also in making decisions throughout our lives that follow from our primary vocational choice. We saw above that vocational discernment is not a solitary enterprise but involves vital connection with the Christian community. As part of that connection, we need the personal guidance of those who have experience in Christian life and ministry. These must be people to whom we can entrust the deepest parts of our souls. Among such mentors, a spiritual director is of particular importance. Spiritual directors walk with us and help us listen to the voice of God as God addresses us in the

events of ordinary life. They are individuals with whom we can
be completely honest without fear of judgment or violation of
confidentiality. They are present to us not so much to instruct us
as to help us get into closer touch with the movements of God in
our lives. Building a strong relationship with a spiritual director
requires a commitment of time and effort, but in the long run it
becomes an invaluable gift as we seek to discern God's will.

Deepening one's knowledge of our faith tradition nourishes a per-
son's discernment of vocation. We have seen that those who engage
in research about young adult Catholics, as well as young adults
themselves, point to the need for more in-depth formation in the
Catholic tradition. If a person makes a decision to enter a program of formation for ministry in the church, further theological
education is required. But even before beginning a structured
program of formation, reading good books in spirituality and
theology, attending lectures and participating in retreats, taking
courses that are available in one's location, and utilizing the
resources of the internet are ways of strengthening one's grasp
of the church's astoundingly rich tradition. This knowledge not
only feeds the mind, it also touches the heart and enriches a
person's prayer and discernment. For example, becoming more
familiar with the lives of people like Augustine, Francis of Assisi, Teresa of Avila, Dorothy Day, and Oscar Romero provides
priceless insights into the ways in which God is present and active in the lives of those whom God calls. While one's personal
journey of faith never simply mirrors that of any other person,
knowledge of the classic stories of our ancestors in the faith helps
us to pay closer attention to God's stirrings in our own lives.

In the current climate, responding to the call to serve as a reli-
gious, priest, or lay ecclesial minister demands courage. Some of the
authors in this book have mentioned the serious struggles that
the church has experienced in recent years: sexual abuse and
financial scandals, polarization between conservatives and liber-
als, diminishment in the numbers of those entering religious life
and priestly formation, and the decline of regular participation
in the life of the church among all age groups, including young
adults. These developments present real challenges to the church

that should not be ignored by any Catholic, especially anyone who is discerning an ecclesial vocation. Young adults who are considering a life of service in the church will undoubtedly encounter people who question the wisdom of such a vocational choice in the wake of these difficulties. Moreover, there are real sacrifices that are entailed in responding to such a call. Foregoing marriage and a family in order to become a religious or priest is not easy, and there are people in our society who claim that it is not a healthy way to live. No lay ecclesial minister is ever going to earn the salary made by an investment banker. At the same time, sacrifice is a part of any vocation that is lived well, and Christians know that Jesus called his disciples to lose their lives in order to gain them. In the history of the church it has been at the very moments of greatest struggle that God has raised up men and women to renew the church and lead God's people into a new springtime. When Saint Francis of Assisi responded to Christ's call to rebuild his church he soon realized that this entailed more than the physical repair of a dilapidated building; it meant a spiritual renewal of God's people grounded in a love for Christ and a deeper appreciation of the Gospel. Donald Senior wrote that this is precisely the time in which we need to dig deep into our heritage and to lift up the noble ideals of our Christian faith. For that to happen, the church needs young adult men and women who will respond courageously to the call to serve the people of God.

Each vocation is a unique mystery. While there are common elements and observable patterns in vocational discernment, every person who seeks to respond to the call is a beloved son or daughter of God with his or her own distinctive story. Many of the saints and mystics have taught that God is closer to us than we are to ourselves. This was their way of testifying to the indescribable nearness of God and to God's intimate knowledge of each one of us. Julian of Norwich, a fourteenth-century English mystic, depicted the closeness of Christ by using the imagery of clothing: "He is our clothing, who wraps and enfolds us for love, embraces and shelters us, surrounds us for his love, which is so tender that he may never desert us."[1] One of the privileges of my life has been the opportunity to read the personal essays of young adults who apply for admission to the Catholics on Call conferences. I am always deeply impressed by the stories of faith and service shared by these men and women. Reading these stories offers a glimpse into the movements of God's grace that have been present and at work in these young adults. While there are discernible patterns in these narratives, each one has its own distinctive plot. In his discussion of the art of discernment, Bishop Morneau shared one of his own poems, "On the Log by the River in the Morning." In that poem he envisions sitting on a log with the divine Master, talking of yesterday's events and planning for today. Every person who seeks to discern a call from God has his or her own "log" on which they are invited to sit and discuss all of the details of their lives with the divine Master. This divine Master speaks his word in the heart of every person in a way that reverences their uniqueness and leads them on their journey one step at a time.

There comes a time in the process of discernment when we have to make the best decision that we can, according to the lights that we have been given. In his wise and helpful discussion of principles of discernment, Bishop Morneau strikes a subtle balance on the question of timing. He counsels his readers to avoid both haste and procrastination. After we have weighed the various options that are available in a context of prayer and dialogue with others, there does come a point when we need to risk a decision. We make such decisions in faith, without the 100 percent certitude that we would like to have. We choose according to the lights that we have been given. There is always risk, but we can take this risk with trust in a faithful God who knows better than we do that we are limited and fallible creatures who are trying to make the best possible decision.

We should approach vocational discernment with trust and hope. Donald Senior reminds us that God through Christ is the source of every vocation; because of this we have solid reasons to hope. Sometimes when we are searching for God's will in our lives that quest can be suffused with great trepidation. We may have doubts about our capacity to discern and respond to what God is asking of us. We may anxiously wonder, what if I make the wrong decision? Or we may liken discernment to figuring out the solution to a difficult, complex problem where part of the evidence is hidden from us. What happens if I give the wrong answer? If that is the way in which we approach discernment it will probably be a frightening and frustrating experience. We need to remember that discernment flows from *relationship*. The God whose word we are striving to hear and obey is the One who created us in order that he might establish with us a relationship of love. This is the God who in Christ poured out his love completely, even to the point of stretching out his arms on a cross. This is the God whom the Scriptures describe as faithful to his people from age to age. In fact, even when they made bad decisions and took wrong turns God remained tenaciously faithful to them. This is the God who turned the nightmare of Calvary into the dawn of Easter by raising Jesus from the dead, by bringing life out of death. Indeed for Christians the life, death, and resurrection of Jesus disclose that this is what God does for a living—God brings life out of the many manifestations of death that we encounter. This conviction is the ultimate source of Christian hope.

In July of 1738 an Italian priest and spiritual director named Paul Danei wrote a letter to a young man who was straining very hard to discern and respond to God's call in his life. Paul Danei would later be known as Saint Paul of the Cross, the founder of the Passionist community and a renowned preacher and mystic. The man to whom he wrote this letter, Francis Appiani, was struggling with his vocation, and he was prone to anxiety and scrupulosity. In his letter Paul of the Cross encouraged Francis to entrust himself to the care of a faithful God:

> Rest yourself with some licit recreation and take the necessary sleep. When you take your solitary walks, listen to the sermon of the flowers, the trees, the bushes, the heavens, the sun, and all the world. You will find they preach of love and praise of God, and invite you to magnify the greatness of the Sovereign Artist, who gave them being. Flee from scruples like the plague.

They cause the soul to lose immense treasures. Pursue the good, entrust yourself to God, and do not try to acquire perfection with the strength of your arms, but proceed as gently as you can. . . . Have no doubt but that God holds you in his divine arms, and that the time will come when he will reveal his Holy Will to you.[2]

While the style and language of this letter bear the marks of eighteenth-century Italian prose, the central message is relevant to people of any century who are engaged in the process of vocational discernment. We can enter into this journey with hope because we entrust ourselves to the God who holds each of us in the divine arms. We can trust that if we sincerely seek to discern and respond to God's will that God will show us the way, that the time will come when God will reveal his will to us. Of that we can be sure.

Notes

Introduction, pages 1–11

1. William D'Antonio, James D. Davidson, Dean R. Hoge, and Mary L. Gautier, *American Catholics Today: New Realities of Their Faith and Their Church* (Lanham, MD: Rowman and Littlefield, 2007), 69, 77–78.

2. Dean R. Hoge and Marti R. Jewell, *Young Adult Catholics and Their Future in Ministry: Interim Report on the 2007 Survey of the Next Generation of Pastoral Leaders* (2007 National Association for Lay Ministry), accessed at http://www.emergingmodels.org/doc/Interim%20Final%20011507.pdf.

3. Tim Muldoon, *Seeds of Hope: Young Adults and the Catholic Church in the United States*, (New York: Paulist Press, 2008), 66.

4. Richard G. Malloy, "Religious Life in the Age of Facebook," *America* 199, no. 1 (July 7–14, 2008): 14–16.

5. Center for Applied Research on the Apostolate, "Recent Vocations to Religious Life: A Report for the National Vocation Religious Conference," accessed at http://www.nrvc.net/index.php?option=com_content&task=view&id=409.

6. Hoge and Jewell, *Young Adult Catholics and Their Future in Ministry*, http://www.emergingmodels.org/doc/Interim%20Final%20011507.pdf.

7. See *Vatican Council II: Volume I, The Conciliar and Post-Conciliar Documents*, ed. Austin Flannery (Northport, NY: Costello Publishing, 1975/1996).

8. Christian Smith, with Patricia Snell, *Souls in Transition: The Religious and Spiritual Lives of Emerging Adults* (Oxford: Oxford University Press, 2009); Robert Wuthnow, *After the Baby Boomers: How Twenty- and Thirty-Somethings Are Shaping the Future of American Religion* (Princeton and Oxford: Princeton University Press, 2007).

9. Smith, *Souls in Transition*, 280.

10. Wuthnow, *After the Baby Boomers*, 232.

Chapter 3, pages 44–62

1. Karl Rahner, "Concerning the Relationship Between Nature and Grace," *Theological Investigations*, vol. 1, trans. Cornelius Ernst (Baltimore: Helicon Press, 1961), 310.

2. Teresa of Avila, *The Book of Her Life: The Collected Works of St. Teresa of Avila*, trans. Kieran Kavanaugh and Otilio Rodriguez (Washington: ICS Publications, 1976), 8, 5; emphasis added.

3. Ibid., 22, 6; emphasis added.

4. Paul Wadell, "Friendship," *The Collegeville Pastoral Dictionary of Biblical Theology*, ed. Carroll Stuhlmueller (Collegeville, MN: Liturgical Press, 1996), 350.

5. Karl Rahner, *On Prayer* (Collegeville, MN: Liturgical Press, 1993), 9.

6. Robert Morneau, *Spiritual Direction: Principles and Practices* (New York: Crossroad, 1996), 12.

7. Rahner, *On Prayer*, 11.

8. Morneau, *Spiritual Direction*, 22.

9. Ibid., 101.

10. Ibid., 16; emphasis in original.

11. Rahner, *On Prayer*, 69–70.

12. Ibid., 70.

13. Ibid., 75.

14. Ibid., 76.

15. Ibid., 78–79.

16. Morneau, *Spiritual Direction*, 35.

Chapter 4, pages 63–81

1. Evelyn Eaton Whitehead and James D. Whitehead, *Christian Life Patterns: The Psychological Challenges and Religious Invitations of Adult Life*. (Garden City, NY: Doubleday, 1982), 21.

2. Jim Wallis, *Call to Conversion* (New York: Harper & Row, 1981), 115.

3. *Mother Teresa, Come Be My Light: The Private Writings of the "Saint of Calcutta,"* ed. Brian Kolodiejchuk (New York: Doubleday, 2007), 44.

4. Gerald O'Collins, *Fundamental Theology* (New York: Paulist Press, 1981), 94–95.

5. Thomas Merton, *Seeds of Contemplation* (New York: Dell Publishing, 1949), 60.

6. Walker Percy, *The Second Coming* (New York: Farrar, Straus, Giroux, 1980), 182.

7. Augustine of Hippo, *Confessions*, trans. Henry Chadwick (Oxford: Oxford University Press, 1991), book 8, 29.

8. John Cassian, *Conferences*, trans. Colm Luibheid (New York: Paulist Press, 1985), 62.

9. Augustine, *Confessions*, book 10, 38.

10. George Eliot, *Adam Bede* (New York: New American Library, 1981), 480.

11. Thomas Green, *Darkness in the Marketplace* (Notre Dame, IN: Ave Maria Press, 1982), 44.

12. V. Therrien, quoted in Yves Congar, *I Believe in the Holy Spirit*, trans. David Smith, vol. 2 (New York: Crossroad, 1997), 180.

13. Thérèse of Lisieux, *Story of a Soul: The Autobiography of Thérèse of Lisieux*, trans. John Clarke (Washington, DC: ICS Publications, 1975), 27.

Chapter 5, pages 82–97

1. See Terrence W. Tilley, *The Disciples' Jesus: Christology as Reconciling Practice* (Maryknoll, NY: Orbis, 2008).

2. Daniel J. Harrington, *God's People in Christ* (Philadelphia: Fortress, 1980), 29.

3. Joseph Ratzinger, *Principles of Catholic Theology* (San Francisco: Ignatius Press, 1987), 53.

4. Gerhard Lohfink, *Does God Need the Church?* (Collegeville, MN: Liturgical Press, 1999), 259–60.

5. Ernst Käsemann, "Paul and Early Catholicism," in *New Testament Questions of Today* (London: SCM Press, 1969), 235–51.

6. Francis A. Sullivan, *The Church We Believe In: One, Holy, Catholic and Apostolic* (New York: Paulist, 1988), 85; J. N. D. Kelly, "'Catholic' and 'Apostolic' in the Early Centuries," *One in Christ* 6 (1970): 278; Augustine, *Cont. ep. Manichaei* 4.5.

7. See Austin Flannery, ed., *Vatican Council II: Volume I, The Conciliar and Post Conciliar Documents* (Northport, NY: Costello Publishing, 1975/1996); the documents of the council are also available on the Vatican web site.

8. Extraordinary Synod of Bishops, "The Final Report," in *Origins* 15 (1985): 449.

9. Karl Rahner, "Towards a Fundamental Theological Interpretation of Vatican Council II," *Theological Studies* 40 (1979): 718.

10. See for example, *From the Pews in the Back: Young Women and Catholicism*, ed. Kate Dugan and Jennifer Owens (Collegeville, MN: Liturgical Press, 2009).

Chapter 6, pages 98–112

1. Congar published an important study of the laity in the church in 1953. For an English translation see *Lay People in the Church* (Westminster, MD: The Newman Press, 1967).

2. See *Vatican Council II: Volume 1, The Conciliar and Post-Conciliar Documents*, ed. Austin Flannery (Northport, NY: Costello Publishing, 1975/1996).

3. Jon Nilson, "The Laity," *The Gift of the Church: A Textbook on Ecclesiology*, ed. Peter Phan (Collegeville, MN: Liturgical Press, 2000), 405–6.

4. United States Conference of Catholic Bishops, Called and Gifted (USCCB Publishing 1980).

5. USCCB, Called and Gifted for the Third Millennium (USCCB Publishing, 1995).

6. Zeni Fox, "Ecclesial Lay Ministers: An Overview," Together in God's Service (USCCB Publishing, 1998).

7. USCCB, Co-Workers in the Vineyard of the Lord: A Resource for Guiding the Development of Lay Ecclesial Ministry, *Origins* 35, no. 25 (December 1, 2005): 405–27.

8. Ibid. 407; see *Novo Millennio Ineunte*, 46.

9. Co-Workers in the Vineyard, 409.

10. Ibid., 416.

11. Ibid., 419.

12. Joseph Cardinal Bernardin, In Service of One Another, *Selected Works of Joseph Cardinal Bernardin*, vol. 1, *Homilies and Teaching Documents* (Collegeville, MN: Liturgical Press, 2000): 27–42.

13. Ibid., 41–42.

14. National Association of Lay Ministry position statement on employment practices. See www.nalm.org.

Chapter 7, pages 113–131

1. Mary Oliver, *New and Selected Poems*, vol. 1 (Boston, MA: Beacon Press, 1992), 94. Used with permission.

2. Sandra Schneiders, *Selling All* (Mahwah, NJ: Paulist Press, 2001), 9.

3. Origin uncertain; attributed to Pedro Arrupe (1907–91), superior general of the Society of Jesus from 1961 to 1984.

4. Carol Scheiber, "A Vocabulary of Vocation," *VISION: The 2008 Annual Religious Vocation Discernment Guide* (Chicago, IL: TrueQuest Communications, 2008), 74.

5. Ibid., 76–77.

6. Judith Merkle, *A Different Touch: A Study of Vows in Religious Life* (Collegeville, MN: Liturgical Press, 1998), 171.

7. Christopher West, *Heaven's Song: Sexual Love as It Was Meant to Be* (West Chester, PA: Ascension Press, 2008), 9.

8. Kathleen Rooney, *Sisters: An Inside Look* (Winona, MN: St. Mary's Press, 2001), 34.

9. *Constitutions of the Sisters of Saint Joseph*, 27–28.

10. Ibid.,16.

11. Editorial, "Generation S," *America* 200, no. 7 (March 2, 2009): 5.

12. Donald Senior, "It All Begins with a Call," *VISION: The 2004 Annual Religious Vocation Discernment Guide* (Chicago, IL: TrueQuest Communications, 2004), 38.

13. St. Augustine of Hippo, *Confessions*, book 1, 1, trans. Maria Boulding (Hyde Park, NY: New City Press, 1997), 39.

14. Warren Sazama, *Discernment of Spirits: A Practical Vocation Guide* (Chicago, IL: National Religious Vocation Conference), 5–10.

15. Ibid., 24.

16. Patrice J. Tuohy, "The Art of Discernment," *Vision: The 2008 Annual Religious Vocation Discernment Guide* (Chicago: TrueQuest Communications, 2008), 142.

17. John Bell, "Will You Come and Follow Me (The Summons)," Copyright © 1987, Wild Goose Resource Group, Iona Community, Scotland. GIA Publications, Inc., exclusive North American agent, 7404 S. Mason Ave., Chicago, IL 60638. www.giamusic.com. 800.442.1358. All rights reserved. Used by permission.

Chapter 8, pages 132–147

1. We usually hear this sacrament referred to as the sacrament of holy orders. More accurate, however, is to speak of the sacrament in the singular (holy order). This is a more accurate translation of the Latin *Sacramentum Ordinis*, and also reflects the theological reality that there is only one sacrament, but with three "grades," or levels of participation. The fullness of the sacrament is found in the episcopacy. Priests and deacons share in various aspects of the bishop's ministry: the priest in the bishop's governing and sacramental ministry, the deacon in the bishop's sacramental ministry and his ministry of service to the poor and needy in the church and the world.

2. In the Latin rite Catholic Church today, ordained ministry is only open to males who will make a commitment to celibacy. There are in fact some priests who are married, but this is an exception in the Latin rite.

3. See the Dogmatic Constitution on the Church (*Lumen Gentium*) in *Vatican Council II: Volume I, The Conciliar and Post-Conciliar Documents*, ed. Austin Flannery (Northport, NY: Costello Publishing, 1975/1996); the document on priesthood from the 1971 Synod of Bishops; and Pope John Paul II, I Will Give You Shepherds (*Pastores Dabo Vobis*).

4. Augustine, Sermon 340, 1 (PL 38, 1483).

5. United States Conference of Catholic Bishops, As One Who Serves (Washington, DC: United States Catholic Conference, 1977).

6. Avery Dulles, "Models of Ministerial Priesthood," *Origins*, 20 (1990): 284–89.

7. Frederick Buechner, *Beyond Words: Daily Readings in the ABCs of Faith*, quoted in William David Thomson, *On-the-Job Prayers: 101 Reflections and Prayers for Christians in Every Occupation* (Skokie, IL: Acta Publications, 2006), 32. Buechner's exact words are "The place God calls you to is the place where your deep gladness and the world's deep hunger meet."

Chapter 9, pages 148–156

1. Julian of Norwich, *Showings*, trans. Edmund Colledge and James Walsh (New York: Paulist Press, 1978), 183.

2. Paul of the Cross, Letter to Francis Appiani, July 16, 1738, in *The Letters of St. Paul of the Cross*, vol. 1, trans. Roger Mercurio and Frederick Sucher, ed. Laurence Finn and Donald Webber (Hyde Park, NY: New City Press, 2000), 235.